Recommended
LITERATURE

Grades
Nine Through Twelve

Publishing Information

Recommended Literature, Grades Nine Through Twelve, was prepared by
the Department of Education's Language Arts and Foreign Languages
Unit, working with two advisory committees (see Acknowledgments). The
document was edited for publication by Mirko Strazicich of the Bureau of
Publications, working cooperatively with Leonard Hull of the Language
Arts and Foreign Languages Unit. It was prepared for photo-offset
production by the staff of the Bureau of Publications, with artwork and
layout by Cheryl Shawver McDonald.

The document was published by the California State Department of Education, 721 Capitol Mall, Sacramento, California (mailing address: P.O.
Box 944272, Sacramento, CA 94244-2720). It was printed by the Office
of State Printing and distributed under the provisions of the Library Distri-
bution Act and *Government Code* Section 11096.

Copies of this publication are available for $4.50 each, plus sales tax for
California residents, from the Bureau of Publications, Sales Unit,
California State Department of Education, P.O. Box 271, Sacramento, CA
95802-0271 (telephone: 916-445-1260). An order form is provided on
page 103 of this publication.

A list of other publications available from the Department of Education
may be found on page 101 of this publication.

ISBN 0-8011-0831-4

Contents

Foreword

*R*ECOMMENDED LITERATURE, GRADES NINE THROUGH TWELVE identifies the great works of literature—literary classics, modern-day classics, and books for recreational reading for high school English–language arts students. I am convinced that great books can touch young people's lives and stimulate their minds and hearts. Every student deserves a chance to explore the challenging storehouse of socially empowering insights and ideas found in high-quality literature.

Literature is the key to successful English–language arts programs for all students, not just the academic elite; and for all educational levels, not just high school. Teaching literature well, however, requires a formidable degree of learning, imagination, and energy.

To assist local school-level planners, I am recommending the books that are listed in this document as examples of good literature for high school students. The more than 1,200 listed titles represent the advisory committee members' best recommendations. I believe that you will find the lists useful as you work to improve your literature program.

Bill Honig

Superintendent of Public Instruction

Preface

THIS publication, *Recommended Literature, Grades Nine Through Twelve*, was compiled by teachers, administrators, curriculum planners, and both public and school librarians from throughout California to (1) encourage students to read and to view reading literature as a worthwhile activity; (2) help local curriculum planners select books for their literature courses; and (3) stimulate educators at the local level to evaluate their literature programs and, if necessary, improve them.

To ensure that *Recommended Literature* would help educators review their literature programs and encourage students to read literature, the compilers formed three working groups—one to formulate a list of readings, another to list readings in languages other than English, and a third to review and refine the lists. Working together for over a year, the groups reviewed several thousand titles. And after many meetings, the members agreed on the more than 1,200 titles listed in this document. These titles represent classical as well as contemporary works of fiction, nonfiction, poetry, and drama. The list also includes works that students whose primary language is other than English can read and enjoy.

We are pleased to present this edition of *Recommended Literature, Grades Nine Through Twelve*. Since the first listing published as part of the *Model Curriculum Standards* in 1985, we have received numerous suggestions for improving the lists. These ideas and comments led to the development of this document.

We give special recognition to Leonard Hull, Consultant (retired), Language Arts and Foreign Languages Unit, and to Ellis Vance, Coordinator of Staff Development, Language Arts and History–Social Science, Clovis Unified School District. Because of their untiring efforts and patience, *Recommended Literature* has become a reality. We are grateful to the educators and librarians whose names appear in the Acknowledgments for developing and producing a document that represents such a wide variety of titles in literature—titles that educators can recommend and students can read with pleasure.

JAMES R. SMITH
Deputy Superintendent
Curriculum and Instructional
    Leadership Branch

FRANCIE ALEXANDER
Associate Superintendent
Curriculum, Instruction, and
    Assessment Division

TOMAS LOPEZ
Director
Office of Humanities
Curriculum Services

SHIRLEY HAZLETT
Manager
Language Arts and
Foreign Languages Unit

Acknowledgments

THIS literature list was prepared with the assistance of two committees composed of school administrators, curriculum planners and consultants, college professors, teachers, and librarians. Superintendent of Public Instruction Bill Honig and members of his staff are most grateful for the efforts and contributions of the members of the two committees, the members of the California Media and Library Educators Association who coordinated the selection of the titles, and the educators and librarians who served on field review groups that responded to the drafts of this document. The members of the committees included the following:

Writing Committee

Stella F. Baker,* Coordinator of Young Adult Services, Contra Costa County Library/BAYA**

Donna Bessant,* District Librarian, Monterey Peninsula Unified School District/ CMLEA**

Beverly Braun, High School Librarian, Monterey Peninsula Unified School District/CMLEA

Marilyn Carpenter,* Education Consultant/CRA**

Fran Claggett,* Education Consultant/CATE**

Joan Curry, Professor of Reading and Language Arts, University of California, San Diego/CRA

Lynn Eisenhut, Coordinator of Children's Services, Orange County Library/ CLA**

Caryn Grossman, Young Adult Manager, Alameda County Library/CLA

Millicent Hill, English Teacher, Crenshaw Senior High School, Los Angeles/ CATE

Barbara Jeffus,* Library Coordinator, Office of the Fresno County Superintendent of Schools/CMLEA

Marilyn D. Kahl, Teacher, West Covina High School/CATE (In memoriam)

Penny Kastanis,* Program Manager, Library Media Services, Office of the Sacramento County Superintendent of Schools/CMLEA

Judy Laird, Teacher, San Juan Unified School District/CMLEA

Jan Lieberman,* Lecturer; and Consultant, San Jose State University and the University of Santa Clara/CMLEA

Walter Loban,* Professor Emeritus, University of California, Berkeley/CATE

Lori Morgan, Reading Department Chairperson, Orange Unified School District/ CRA

---

*Special consultant for the project.
**BAYA—Bay Area Young Adult Librarians
  CATE—California Association of Teachers of English
  CLA—California Library Association
  CMLEA—California Media and Library Educators Association
  CRA—California Reading Association

Kathleen Naylor, Consultant and Author/CATE

Kay Niemeyer, County Media Director, Office of the San Diego County Superintendent of Schools/CMLEA

Jesse Perry, Program Manager, English/Language Arts, San Diego City Unified School District/CATE

Cherri Sakamoto, Librarian, Los Angeles Unified School District/CMLEA

Cathy Saldin, Public Librarian, West Covina Library/CLA

Barbara Swanson, Coordinator of Children's Services, Kern County Library/CLA

William H. Thomas,* Curriculum Specialist, Mount Diablo Unified School District/CATE

Judith Toll,* Librarian, San Leandro High School/CMLEA

Jan Van Meter,* English Teacher, Roosevelt High School, Fresno/CATE

W. Jean Wickey,* Teacher/Librarian, Bakersfield City Elementary School District/CMLEA

Norma Willson,* Curriculum Consultant, Torrance Unified School District/CATE

Barbara Zussman,* English Teacher; and Language Arts Subject Area Specialist, Beverly Hills Unified School District/CATE

Special Committee to Select Books in Languages Other Than English

Carol Y. Bowen, Member, California Indian Education Association

Maria Guadalupe Canales, Teacher, Norwalk-La Mirada Unified School District

Setsuko Chiba, Instructor, California State University, Sacramento

Chiung-Sally Chou, Secondary ESL/Bilingual Program Specialist, Alhambra City High School District

Florence Hongo, President of the Board and Manager, Japanese-American Curriculum Project

Judy Lewis, Transition English Program Facilitator, Folsom-Cordova Unified School District

Alicia Lloreda, English Teacher, Schurr High School, Montebello

Walter Loban, Professor Emeritus, University of California, Berkeley

Marisol Naso, Bilingual Education Coordinator, San Bernardino City Unified School District

Mory Ouk, Instructional Associate for LEP Services, Long Beach Unified School District

Clara Park, Program Specialist (Bilingual), Torrance Unified School District

Tracey Petre, English Teacher, Carson Senior High School, Los Angeles

Kim-Anh Nguyen Phan, Coordinator of Indochinese Programs, San Jose Unified School District

Corazon A. Ponce, Program Administrator, San Francisco Unified School District

Alice Scofield, Professor, San Jose State University

Juan C. Vallejo, Lecturer, University of California, Davis; and President, Language Dynamics

Lue Vang, Transition Program Specialist, Folsom-Cordova Unified School District

Pamela Vasquez, Bilingual/ESL Specialist, Glendale Unified School District

Glorianna Y. Whaley, Member, California Indian Education Association

Special Acknowledgments

Computer programmer for the project: **Janet Harwell,** Clovis Unified School District
Compiler: **Leonard Hull,** Consultant (retired), Language Arts and Foreign Languages Unit, State Department of Education
Committee coordinator for CMLEA: **Ellis Vance,** Coordinator of Staff Development, Language Arts and History/Social Science, Clovis Unified School District
Computer programmer for the project: **Linda Vocal,** Office of Humanities Curriculum Services, State Department of Education

State Department of Education Staff Members

William Adorno, Assistant Manager, Bilingual Education Office
Hector Burke, Consultant, Bilingual Education Office
Catharine Farrell, Zellerbach Family Fund Consultant attached to the Language Arts and Foreign Languages Unit
Eva Fong, Consultant, External Affairs Office
Mae Gundlach, Consultant, Language Arts and Foreign Languages Unit
Shirley Hazlett, Manager, Language Arts and Foreign Languages Unit
Van Le, Consultant, Bilingual Education Office
Robert Lee, Consultant, Bilingual Education Office
Adele Martinez, Consultant, Language Arts and Foreign Languages Unit

State Department of Education Support Staff

Diane Davis, Office of Humanities Curriculum Services
Gerin Pebbles, Language Arts and Foreign Languages Unit
Dolores Vidales, Office of Humanities Curriculum Services

Introduction

APRIMARY goal for teaching literature is for students to discover the pleasure and the illumination that a fine piece of literature offers. Another significant goal is for students to become lifelong readers of literature. Through the reading of literature, students may experience vicariously the lives of others, different time periods, places, value systems, and the many cultures of the world.

This document contains recommended readings for students in grades nine through twelve. Local educators are encouraged to use these recommendations when reviewing their English language arts curriculum and when selecting literature to implement that curriculum.

Basic Intent of This Document

This list of reading materials is intended only as a guide for local-level policymakers, curriculum planners, teachers, and librarians; *it is not intended to be prescriptive in any way.* Local educators should encourage parents to become involved in the selection process of literature for the core program and for the independent reading program. Finally, this document is intended to encourage educators to review their literature programs and the accompanying instructional materials.

Development of the List

The development of the list involved many educators and librarians who used many reference resources as well as their own experience at all levels. Under the auspices of the California Media and Library Educators Association, a writing committee was established to select the titles for a base list that was validated by a large group of field responders. The list of books in languages other than English was developed by educators and teachers who are currently working and teaching in other than English language literature programs. This list also was validated by a large group of field responders. This document was then developed by California educators for use by planners, teachers, and librarians in the secondary schools.

Local Decision-making Processes and Materials Selection Policies

This document is a resource that reflects the ideas of thoughtful educators from around the state. However, decisions about local programs and materials for those programs must be made at the local level. To make these local decisions, each school or school district should have a materials selection policy that guides the purchase of materials for instruction and for school and classroom libraries. This policy should include a provision for a materials selection committee that, at the minimum, includes in its membership administrators, curriculum planners, librarians, classroom teachers, and community representatives.

Format of This Document

When selecting the format for this document, the developers were guided by one objective: to make the document easy to understand and to use. To accomplish this objective, the committee decided to:

1. Divide the list into two sections that would cover all the entries. The sections are "Core and Extended Materials" and "Recreational and Motivational Materials."
2. List the titles within these sections by traditional categories that are generally well-known by high school teachers. The categories are:

    Biographies
    Drama
    Folklore, Mythology, and Epics
    Nonfiction, Essays, and Speeches
    Novels
    Poetry
    Short Stories
    Books in Languages Other Than English

3. List each entry alphabetically by author or by title if it has no author. (Publishers are not cited.)
4. Use a matrix to give helpful information that will assist local selectors of titles when searching for or selecting books.
5. Provide an index of authors and titles at the end of the document.
6. Include an appendix dealing with storytelling.

When teachers, librarians, and program planners use the lists, they will have a matrix with special information to assist them. Many educators will not need to use the matrix but, for those who do, the columns have been designed accordingly:

1. Core and extended materials are designated by using the letters *C* and *E*.
2. The grade spans have been suggested by the committee members and are not prescriptive in any way. Local educators may opt to introduce certain works at different levels.
3. The literary contributions of specific ethnic or cultural groups are identified by one of the following symbols:

    B—Black   J—Japanese
    C—Chinese   K—Korean
    F—Filipino   Kh—Khmer
    H—Hispanic   S—Samoan
    Hm—Hmong   V—Vietnamese
    I—American Indian

The literature of these ethnic groups has been identified because it can be used by students in their literature programs to better understand the many cultural groups of students represented in California high schools.

Terms Used

In the lists that follow, titles are classified as core (C) literature, extended (E) literature, or recreational/motivational (R/M) literature. This classification is used to assist local educators as they develop their programs and compile their own lists. The three types of literature are defined as follows:

Core literature. Core literature includes those selections that are to be *taught* in the classroom, are given close reading and intensive consideration, and are likely to be an important stimulus for writing and discussion. The core list should contain works of compelling, intellectual, social, or moral content. The core literature must be examples of excellent language use. District materials selection committees develop the basic list of core titles that teachers use in their classes.

Extended literature. Extended literature includes works that a teacher may assign to individual students or small groups of students to read for homework or individual reading to supplement classwork. Literature in the extended list also has emotional, aesthetic substance.

Recreational/motivational literature. Teachers and librarians should suggest recreational/motivational works to guide students when they are selecting individual, leisure-time reading materials from classroom, school, and community libraries. This type of literature may include works of special appeal to individual readers as well as works of universal appeal to all students.

Literature for Students in Grades Nine Through Twelve

The recommended readings listed in this document are for students in grades nine through twelve. Works in eight categories have been chosen to accommodate a variety of tastes, abilities, and learning modalities. The selections include works about other cultures and works by authors that contribute to our common culture; works written or translated into languages other than English for students who read another language better than they do English; the classics, including modern-day classics; and just good reading materials for students to enjoy.

This list of recommended literature is a resource that high school teachers and their curriculum planners may use to develop a literature program that has both scope and sequence. It is important that students at each grade level have experience with literature of a number of types and genres. They should be reading and hearing literature of all the genres. Their experiences should include materials from the oral tradition, such as folklore and myth, modern fantasy, realistic adventure, and historical fiction. As students read and respond to literature regularly and systematically, they will be improving their thinking processes, critical reading skills, and the ability to interpret and explain what is written. As students participate in imaginative writing activities, their interest in reading literature will be enhanced.

As the literature program is developed, curriculum planners must be careful to include materials from varied cultures. Because these materials contribute to understanding and mutual respect, they are as important for members of nonminority groups as for those in the minority groups. This list includes and identifies such literature.

If a program of literature is to succeed, parental cooperation is very important. The recreational reading usually takes place outside the school setting, and encouragement and interest demonstrated by family members can reinforce what the school is saying about the importance and value of reading literature. Thus, when the program is being initiated, advisory groups of parents and other community members can help with the school-home communication.

Literature for All Students

The literature program is for all students. Those who cannot yet read English can read books in their first languages. While primary emphasis in a literature program is on reading, important adjuncts to the curriculum are films, videotapes and audiotapes, dramatic presentations, and above all, the teacher's systematic reading to the students. The most able readers as well as the least able readers benefit from hearing good literature read aloud.

The love of reading is one of the most important gifts that teachers and parents may give to children. Literature will provide experiences that are ordinarily inaccessible to students, broaden their knowledge of the world and its people, and improve reading skills. Literature is one of the basics and should be taught in all curricular areas.

CORE AND EXTENDED MATERIALS

THIS section contains lists of core and extended materials. It is designed to suggest works to teachers and members of district materials selection committees. For easier use, the entries are divided by categories; a matrix is provided to give users some information about the listed works.

The categories are Biographies; Drama; Folklore, Mythology, and Epics; Nonfiction, Essays, and Speeches; Novels; Poetry; Short Stories; and Books in Languages Other Than English.

The columns of the matrix indicate the type of entry, such as core (C) or extended (E) (see definitions in the Introduction to this document), and the grade span where the work should be introduced. When the entry concerns literary contributions of specific ethnic or cultural groups, the ethnic or cultural group is indicated (see the Introduction for a listing of the groups).

Because of space constraints, it is not possible to list all the works of most of the authors. Consequently, the committee members decided to list only one work per author in most cases. This one work is either the author's acknowledged best work or one of the best. Therefore, when selecting an author's work, the teacher or librarian may wish to search beyond the one work listed before making a final choice.

Biographies

A BIOGRAPHY is a story centering on a person who actually existed or exists. It may tell the story of his or her life in part or in its entirety. Biographies often express themes dealing with a struggle for success with an emphasis on the strength and moral fiber of the subject.

The three essential ingredients of a good biography are history, the person, and literary artistry. The facts should be authentic, objective, and verifiable; the person should be portrayed as a believable individual rather than as a glorified personage; and the writing should be a work of literary art. Although the story of a person's life provides the facts, the writer interprets, selects, and organizes elements to create an aesthetic work.

A good biography can provide a model and help shape the reader's ideals. It can stimulate a reader to copy men and women who are heroes. A biography also can show how human emotions are constant through changing times and customs.

It is impossible to predict the ways in which vivid stories of people might affect the lives of people reading the stories. And there is little the author or teacher can do to mold biographical data or historical fact in plastic, moralistic lessons. The material of biography is as untidy as the unsifted facts of history. A biography often defies the writer's efforts to make sense of it and often leaves the reader curious and questioning. What could be more valuable than that?

Material	Type of entry	Grade span	Culture
Anderson, Marian *My Lord, What a Morning: An Autobiography*	C	9-11	B
Angelou, Maya *I Know Why the Caged Bird Sings*	C	10-12	B
Atkinson, Linda *In Kindling Flame: The Story of Hannah Senesh*	E	9-11	
Baker, Russell *Growing up*	E	9-12	
Beal, Merrill D. *I Will Fight No More Forever: Chief Joseph and the Nez Perce War*	C	9-11	I

Material	Type of entry	Grade span	Culture
Bennett, Lerone, Jr. *What Manner of Man: A Biography of Martin Luther King, Jr.*	E	9-11	B
Bober, Natalie S. *Restless Spirit: The Story of Robert Frost*	C	9-12	
Brown, Claude *Manchild in the Promised Land*	C	10-12	B
Buck, Pearl S. *My Several Worlds: A Personal Record*	E	9-12	
Bulosan, Carlos *America Is in the Heart: A Personal History*	C	10-12	F
Cheever, Susan *Home Before Dark*	E	10-12	
Chu, Louis *Eat a Bowl of Tea*	C	10-12	C
Dana, Richard H., Jr. *Two Years Before the Mast*	E	10-12	
Debo, Angie *Geronimo: The Man, His Time, His Place*	E	10-12	I
Dillard, Annie *An American Childhood*	E	10-12	
Dinesen, Isak *Out of Africa*	C	10-12	
Douglass, Frederick *Narrative of the Life of Frederick Douglass, An American Slave*	C	9-11	B
Eaton, Jeanette *Gandhi: Fighter Without a Sword*	E	9-12	
Frank, Anne *Anne Frank: Diary of a Young Girl*	C	9-11	
Franklin, Benjamin *Autobiography of Benjamin Franklin*	C	10-12	
Freedman, Russell *Lincoln: A Photobiography*	C	9-11	
Galarza, Ernesto *Barrio Boy*	C	9-11	H

Material	Type of entry	Grade span	Culture
Gibson, Althea *I Always Wanted to Be Somebody*	E	9-12	B
Gilchrist, Ellen *Falling Through Space: The Journals of Ellen Gilchrist*	E	10-12	
Gillenkirk, Jeff, and James Motlow *Bitter Melon: Stories from the Last Rural Chinese Town in America*	C	9-12	C
Gunther, John *Death Be Not Proud: A Memoir*	C	9-11	
Guthrie, Woody *Bound for Glory*	E	10-12	
Hamilton, Virginia *W.E.B. Du Bois: A Biography*	E	9-11	B
Hansberry, Lorraine *To Be Young, Gifted and Black*	C	10-12	B
Hautzig, Esther *Endless Steppe: Growing up in Siberia*	E	9-11	
Hellman, Lillian *Three: An Unfinished Woman, Pentimento, Scoundrel Time*	E	10-12	
Herriott, James *All Creatures Great and Small*	C	9-11	
Houston, Jeanne W., and James D. Houston *Farewell to Manzanar*	C	9-11	J
Hurston, Zora Neale *Dust Tracks on a Road: An Autobiography*	E	10-12	B
Hyun, Peter *Man Sei! The Making of a Korean American*	E	9-12	K
Johnson, Dorothy M. *Warrior for a Lost Nation: A Biography of Sitting Bull*	C	10-12	I
Jordan, Barbara, and Shelby Hearon *Barbara Jordan: A Self-Portrait*	E	9-11	B
Keller, Helen *Story of My Life*	C	9-11	
Kennedy, John F. *Profiles in Courage*	E	9-11	

Material	Type of entry	Grade span	Culture
Kherdian, David *Road from Home: The Story of an Armenian Girl*	C	9-11	
Kikumura, Akemi *Through Harsh Winters: The Life of a Japanese Immigrant Woman*	E	9-12	J
Kingston, Maxine Hong *Woman Warrior: Memoirs of a Girlhood Among Ghosts*	C	10-12	C
Kroeber, Theodora *Ishi, Last of His Tribe*	C	9-12	I
Lindbergh, Charles A. *The Spirit of St. Louis*	E	9-11	
Malcolm X *Autobiography of Malcolm X*	C	10-12	B
Markham, Beryl *West with the Night*	E	10-12	
McFadden, Cyra *Rain or Shine: A Family Memoir*	E	9-11	
Mead, Margaret *Blackberry Winter: My Earlier Years*	E	10-12	
Moody, Anne *Coming of Age in Mississippi: An Autobiography*	E	10-12	B
Muir, John *My First Summer in the Sierra*	E	10-12	
Neihardt, John G. *Black Elk Speaks: Being the Life Story of a Holy Man of the Oglala Sioux*	E	9-12	I
Ortiz, Victoria *Sojourner Truth*	E	9-11	B
Petry, Ann *Harriet Tubman: Conductor on the Underground Railroad*	E	9-11	B
Rawlings, Marjorie K. *Cross Creek*	E	10-12	
Rodriquez, Richard *Hunger of Memory: An Autobiography*	E	10-12	

Material	Type of entry	Grade span	Culture
Roosevelt, Eleanor *This I Remember*	E	9-11	
Rowse, Alfred L. (Ed.) *William Shakespeare: A Biography*	E	9-12	
Russel, Bill *Go up for Glory*	E	9-12	B
Sandburg, Carl *Abraham Lincoln: The Prairie Years*	C	10-12	
Soto, Gary *Living up the Street*	E	9-11	H
Soyinka, Wole *Ake: The Years of Childhood*	E	10-12	B
Sullivan, Tom, and Derek L. Gill *If You Could See What I Hear*	E	9-11	
Szymusiak, Molyda *The Stones Cry Out: A Cambodian Childhood*	C	9-11	Kh
T'ai-t'ai, Ning L., and Ida Pruitt *A Daughter of Han: The Autobiography of a Chinese Working Woman*	E	10-12	C
Uchida, Yoshiko *Desert Exile: The Uprooting of a Japanese-American Family*	E	9-11	J
Washington, Booker T. *Up from Slavery*	E	10-12	B
Welty, Eudora *One Writer's Beginnings*	C	10-12	
Wiesel, Elie *Night*	C	9-11	
Wong, Jade Snow *Fifth Chinese Daughter*	E	9-11	C
Wright, Richard *Black Boy: A Record of Childhood and Youth*	C	10-12	B
Yamasaki, Minoru *A Life in Architecture*	E	9-12	J
Yoshikawa, Eiji *Musashi*	E	10-12	J

Drama

THROUGH a rich variety of dramatic works, presented in theater as well as by videotapes, audiotapes, records, disks, and so forth, students have opportunities to explore powerful expressions of the human condition in many cultures and times. Through tragedy, comedy, and fantasy, they experience the problems, the joys, and the dreams of women and men, girls and boys, through the ages. They have opportunities to develop oral fluency and other dramatic skills as they interpret roles; develop writing skills as they write about theme, characters, settings, and literary techniques; or create their own dialogues and plays.

Material	Type of entry	Grade span	Culture
Aeschylus *Oresteian Trilogy*	C	10-12	
Albee, Edward *American Dream and Zoo Story*	C	10-12	
Allen, Woody *Play It Again, Sam*	E	10-12	
Anderson, Robert *I Never Sang for My Father*	C	10-12	
Anouilh, Jean *Antigone*	C	10-12	
Baldwin, James *Amen Corner*	E	10-12	B
Beckett, Samuel *Waiting for Godot*	C	10-12	
Bolt, Robert *A Man for All Seasons*	C	10-12	
Brecht, Bertolt *Mother Courage and Her Children*	C	10-12	
Chekhov, Anton P. *The Cherry Orchard*	C	10-12	

Material	Type of entry	Grade span	Culture
Chin, Frank *The Chickencoop Chinaman and The Year of the Dragon: Two Plays*	C	10-12	C
Davis, Ossie *Purlie*	E	9-12	B
Elder, Lonne *Ceremonies in Dark Old Men*	C	10-12	B
Euripides *Medea*	C	10-12	
Fugard, Athol *Master Harold and the Boys*	C	10-12	B
Garcia Lorca, Federico *Blood Wedding*	C	10-12	H
Gardner, Herb *A Thousand Clowns*	E	9-12	
Gibson, William *Miracle Worker*	C	9-11	
Gilroy, Frank *David and Lisa*	E	10-12	
Glaspell, Susan *Trifles*	E	9-11	
Goodrich, Frances, and Albert Hackett *Diary of Anne Frank*	C	9-11	
Hansberry, Lorraine *Raisin in the Sun*	C	9-12	B
Hellman, Lillian *The Little Foxes*	C	10-12	
Ibsen, Henrik *A Doll's House*	C	10-12	
Ionesco, Eugene *Rhinoceros*	C	10-12	
Izumo, Takeda *Chushingura*	E	10-12	J

Material	Type of entry	Grade span	Culture
Lawrence, Jerome, and Robert E. Lee *The Night Thoreau Spent in Jail*	C	10-12	
Luce, William *Belle of Amherst*	E	10-12	
Lum, Wing Tek *Oranges Are Lucky*	C	10-12	C
McCullers, Carson *The Member of the Wedding*	C	10-12	
Medoff, Mark *Children of a Lesser God*	C	10-12	
Miller, Arthur *The Crucible*	C	10-12	
Norton, Carlos *Meeting*	E	9-12	H
O'Neill, Eugene *Long Day's Journey into Night*	C	10-12	
O Yong-Jin and others *Wedding Day and Other Korean Plays*	C	9-12	K
Pomerance, Bernard *The Elephant Man*	E	10-12	
Rose, Reginald *Twelve Angry Men*	C	10-12	
Rostand, Edmond *Cyrano de Bergerac*	C	10-12	
Sakamoto, Edward *In the Alley*	C	10-12	J
Serling, Rod *Requiem for a Heavyweight*	E	9-11	
Shakespeare, William *Selected Works*	C	9-12	
Shange, Ntozake *For Colored Girls Who Have Considered Suicide When the Rainbow Is Enuf*	E	10-12	B

Material	Type of entry	Grade span	Culture
Shaw, George Bernard *Pygmalion*	C	10-12	
Simon, Neil *Brighton Beach Memoirs*	E	10-12	
Sophocles *Oedipus Trilogy*	C	10-12	
Soyinka, Wole *Opera Wonyosi*	E	10-12	B
Stoppard, Tom *Rosencrantz and Guildenstern Are Dead*	E	10-12	
Thomas, Dylan *Under Milk Wood: A Play for Voices*	C	10-12	
Valdez, Luis *Zoot Suit*	C	9-12	H
Vidal, Gore *A Visit to a Small Planet*	C	9-11	
Wagner, Jane *The Search for Signs of Intelligent Life in the Universe*	E	10-12	
Wasserman, Dale; Mitch Leigh; and Joe Darion *One Flew over the Cuckoo's Nest*	E	10-12	
Wilde, Oscar *The Importance of Being Earnest*	E	10-12	
Wilder, Thornton *Our Town*	C	9-12	
Williams, Tennessee *The Glass Menagerie*	C	10-12	
Wilson, August *Fences*	C	10-12	B
Zindel, Paul *The Effect of Gamma Rays on Man-in-the-Moon Marigolds*	E	9-11	

Folklore, Mythology, and Epics

FOLKLORE, mythology, and epics, like other literary genre, serve as mirrors of the human condition. By their very nature folklore, mythology, and epics reveal people's efforts to explain the uncertainties of nature, human relationships, desires, and fears.

Folklore, mythology, and epics have no boundaries; they all, regardless of ethnicity or religion, have a story to tell. These literary genre have served as an important vehicle for transmitting the cultural, religious, and social mores of a people. By reading and studying them, students can experience those aspects of life that define us as human beings—good, evil, fear, courage, wisdom, weakness, and strength.

Material	Type of entry	Grade span	Culture
Aesop Fables	C	9-12	
Andersen, Hans Christian *Tales and Stories by Hans Christian Andersen*	C	9-12	
Asbjornsen, Peter C. *Norwegian Folktales*	E	9-12	
Beowulf *Beowulf*	C	9-12	
Bierhorst, John (Ed.) *The Hungry Woman: Myths and Legends of the Aztecs*	E	9-12	I/H
Bulfinch, Thomas *Bulfinch's Mythology: The Age of Fable*	C	9-12	
Calvino, Italo *Italian Folktales*	E	9-12	
Carrison, Muriel *Cambodian Folk Stories from the Gatiloke*	E	9-10	Kh
Coburn, Jewell R., and Quyen Van Duong *Beyond the East Wind: Legends and Folktales of Vietnam*	C	9-12	V

Material	Type of entry	Grade span	Culture
Garner, John C. *Grendel*	E	11-12	
Graham, Gail B. *The Beggar in the Blanket*	E	9-12	V
Graves, Robert *Greek Gods and Heroes*	C	9-12	
Griego, José *Cuentos: Tales from the Hispanic Southwest*	E	9-12	H/I
Grimm, Jacob, and Wilhelm K. Grimm *The Juniper Tree and Other Tales from Grimm*	C	9-12	
Hamilton, Edith *Mythology*	C	9-12	
Hamilton, Virginia *The People Could Fly*	C	9-12	B
Haviland, Virginia *North American Legends*	C	9-12	I
Homer *The Iliad*	C	9-12	
Homer *The Odyssey*	C	9-12	
Jacobs, Joseph *English Fairy Tales*	E	9-12	
Jaffrey, Madhur *Seasons of Splendor: Tales, Myths, and Legends from India*	E	9-12	
Jagendorf, Moritz A., and R.S. Boggs *King of the Mountains: A Treasury of Latin-American Folk Stories*	C	9-12	H
Kendall, Carol, and Li Yao-wen *Sweet and Sour: Tales from China*	C	9-12	C
Kroeber, Theodora *The Inland Whale: Nine Stories Retold from California Indian Legends*	E	9-12	I
Kuo, Yuan Hsi, and Louise Hsi Kuo *Chinese Folktales*	E	9-12	C

Material	Type of entry	Grade span	Culture
Leeming, David Adams *Mythology: The Voyage of the Hero*	C	9-12	
Lester, Julius *The Knee-High Man and Other Tales*	E	9-12	B
Liyi, He *The Spring of Butterflies: And Other Chinese Folktales*	E	9-12	C
Lurie, Alison *Clever Gretchen and Other Forgotten Folktales*	E	9-12	
Mackenzie, Donald A. *Myths and Legends of China and Japan*	E	9-12	C/J
Marriott, Alice, and Carol K. Rachlin *American Indian Mythology*	E	9-12	I
Martin, Rafe *Hungry Tigress and Other Traditional Asian Tales*	C	9-12	
McKinley, Robin *Beauty: A Retelling of the Story of Beauty and the Beast*	E	9-12	
Moyle, Richard *Fagogo*	E	10-12	S
O'Brien, Edna *Tales for the Telling: Irish Folk and Fairy Stories*	E	9-12	
Ovid *Metamorphoses*	C	9-12	
Perrault, Charles *Perrault's Complete Fairy Tales*	C	9-12	
Phelps, Ethel J. *Maid of the North: Feminist Folktales from Around the World*	E	9-12	
Ransome, Arthur *War of the Birds and the Beasts and Other Russian Tales*	E	9-12	
Riordan, James *The Woman in the Moon: And Other Tales of Forgotten Heroines*	E	9-12	
Roberts, Moss (Ed.) *Chinese Fairy Tales and Fantasies*	E	9-12	C

Material	Type of entry	Grade span	Culture
Rosenberg, Donna *World Mythology*	C	9-12	
Schultz, George *Vietnamese Legends*	C	9-12	V
Schwartz, Howard *Elijah's Violin and Other Jewish Fairy Tales*	E	9-12	
Seros, Kathleen *Sun and Moon: Fairy Tales from Korea*	E	9-12	K
Singer, Isaac Bashevis *When Shlemiel Went to Warsaw and Other Stories*	E	9-12	
Steinbeck, John *Acts of King Arthur and His Noble Knights*	C	9-12	
Timpanelli, Gioi *Tales from the Roof of the World: Folktales of Tibet*	E	9-12	C
Uchida, Yoshiko *The Dancing Kettle*	E	9-12	J
Virgil *The Aeneid*	C	9-12	
Vuong, Lynette D. *The Brocaded Slipper and Other Vietnamese Tales*	E	9-12	V
Warner, Elizabeth *Heroes, Monsters and Other Worlds from Russian Mythology*	E	9-12	
Werner, E., and T. Chalmers *Ancient Tales and Folklore of China*	E	9-12	C
White, Terence H. *Once and Future King*	C	9-12	
Wigginton, Eliot (Ed.) *Foxfire Book: Hog Dressing, Log Cabin Building, Mountain Crafts and Foods, Planting by the Signs, Snake Lore, Hunting Tales, Faith Healing, Moonshining and Other Affairs of Plain Living*	C	9-12	
Wolkstein, Diane (Ed.) *The Magic Orange Tree: And Other Haitian Folktales*	E	9-12	B
Yolen, Jane (Ed.) *Favorite Folktales from Around the World*	C	9-12	

Nonfiction, Essays, and Speeches

A S students grow and develop, their powers of observation also grow and develop and they see the world around them as a vast area of exploration and discovery. One of the most significant characteristics of a child's mind is curiosity. The fundamental role of nonfiction books, essays, and speeches is to provide students with a body of information that answers old questions but also stimulates the asking of new questions. Such materials should not only explain the many areas of interest to students but also provide the explanation that young minds will find satisfying. Certain criteria must be followed when evaluating these works, such as accuracy, currency, organization and scope, format, and author's competence. However, nonfiction books, essays, and speeches might also be considered fine literature when they fulfill the additional qualities of originality and style of presentation.

Material	Classification*	Type of entry	Grade span	Culture
Baldwin, James *Notes of a Native Son*	E	C	10-12	B
Beal, Merrill D. *I Will Fight No More Forever: Chief Joseph and the Nez Perce War*	E	C	9-12	I
Bronowski, Jacob *Science and Human Values*	NF	C	10-12	
Brown, Dee *Bury My Heart at Wounded Knee: An Indian History of the American West*	NF	C	10-12	I
Brown, John "John Brown's Body" (last speech)	S	E	9-12	
Buchwald, Art *You Can Fool All of the People All of the Time*	E	E	9-12	
Camus, Albert *Myth of Sisyphus*	E	C	10-12	
Capote, Truman *In Cold Blood*	NF	E	10-12	

*E=essay; NF=nonfiction; and S=speech.

Material	Classifi-cation	Type of entry	Grade span	Culture
Carson, Rachel *Silent Spring*	NF	C	9-11	
Cartmail, Keith St. *Exodus Indochina*	NF	C	9-12	V
Chan, Jeffery, and others (Eds.) *Fifty Years of Our Whole Voice*	NF	C	10-12	C/J
Chang, Diana *Woolgathering*	E	C	10-12	C
Chief Joseph "From Where the Sun Now Stands"	S	C	9-12	I
Churchill, Winston "Blood, Sweat, and Tears"	S	C	10-12	
Cleaver, Eldridge *The White Race and Its Heroes*	E	E	10-12	B

Cruz, Juana Inés de la
*Against the Inconsequence of Men's Desires and
   Their Censure of Women for Faults Which They
   Themselves Have Caused*
	E	C	9-12	H

Culley, Margo (Ed.) *A Day at a Time: The Diary Literature of American Women from 1764 to the Present*	NF	E	10-12	
Declaration of Independence of the United States of America	E	C	9-12	
Deloria, Vine, Jr. *Custer Died for Your Sins: An Indian Manifesto*	NF	C	10-12	I
Didion, Joan *Slouching Towards Bethlehem*	E	E	10-12	
Dillard, Annie *Pilgrim at Tinker Creek*	E	C	10-12	
Du Bois, W.E.B. *Souls of Black Folk: Essays and Sketches*	E	C	9-12	B
Duncan, Robert *Truth and Life of Myth*	NF	E	10-12	

Material	Classifi-cation	Type of entry	Grade span	Culture
Dwyer, Robert *Chicano Voices*	E	C	9-12	H
Eiseley, Loren *Star Thrower*	E	C	10-12	
Ellison, Ralph *Going to the Territory*	E	E	10-12	B
Emerson, Ralph Waldo *Self-Reliance*	E	C	10-12	
Ephron, Nora *Crazy Salad Plus Nine*	E	E	10-12	
Faderman, Lillian, and Barbara Bradshaw *Speaking for Ourselves: American Ethnic Writing*	E	C	9-12	B/H/J/I
Faulkner, William Nobel acceptance speech	S	C	10-12	
Fisher, Ann R. *Exile of a Race*	NF	C	9-12	J
Goodman, Ellen *Keeping in Touch*	E	E	9-11	
Gould, Stephen Jay *The Panda's Thumb: More Reflections in Natural History*	NF	C	10-12	
Henry, Patrick "Give Me Liberty or Give Me Death"	S	C	9-12	
Hersey, John *Hiroshima*	NF	C	9-12	
Highwater, Jamake *Many Smokes, Many Moons*	NF	E	9-12	I
Houston, James, and Jeanne W. Houston *Beyond Manzanar and Other Views of Asian-American Womanhood*	E	E	9-12	J
Keillor, Garrison *Lake Wobegon Days*	NF	E	9-12	
Kennedy, John F. "Inaugural Address by John F. Kennedy"	S	C	9-11	

Material	Classifi- cation	Type of entry	Grade span	Culture
Killens, John O. *Negroes Have a Right to Fight Back*	E	E	9-11	B
King, Martin Luther, Jr. "I Have a Dream"	S	C	9-12	B
King, Martin Luther, Jr. *Letter from a Birmingham Jail*	E	C	9-12	B
Kubler-Ross, Elizabeth *On Death and Dying*	NF	E	9-12	
Lamb, Charles *Dissertation on Roast Pig*	E	C	10-12	
Lester, Julius *To Be a Slave*	NF	C	9-11	B
Lilienthal, David "My Faith in Democracy"	S	C	10-12	
Lincoln, Abraham "Gettysburg Address"	S	C	9-12	
Lopez, Barry H. *River Notes: The Dance of the Herons*	E	C	10-12	
Machiavelli, Niccolo *The Prince*	E	C	10-12	
Mannes, Marya "Packaged Deception"	S	E	10-12	
McPhee, John *Coming into the Country*	NF	E	9-12	
Meltzer, Milton *Never to Forget: The Jews of the Holocaust*	NF	E	9-12	
Merriam, Eve *Growing up Female in America: Ten Lives*	NF	E	9-12	
Merriam, Eve, and Nancy Larrick (Eds.) *Male and Female Under Eighteen*	NF	E	9-12	
Meyer, Carolyn *Voices of South Africa: Growing up in a Troubled Land*	NF	E	9-12	

Material	Classifi-cation	Type of entry	Grade span	Culture
Miyasaki, Gail Y. *Obachan*	E	E	9-11	J
Momaday, N. Scott *The Way to Rainy Mountain*	E	C	9-12	I
Neruda, Pablo Nobel acceptance speech	S	C	10-12	H
Newhouse, Nancy R. (Ed.) *Hers—Through Women's Eyes: Essays from "Hers"* *Column of the New York Times*	E	E	10-12	
Ortego, Philip *We Are Chicanos: An Anthology of Chicano Literature*	E	C	9-12	H
Paine, Thomas *Common Sense*	E	C	10-12	
Pirsig, Robert M. *Zen and the Art of Motorcycle Maintenance: An Inquiry* *into Values*	NF	E	10-12	
Plato *The Republic*	E	C	10-12	
Rooney, Andrew *Word for Word*	E	E	9-12	
Royko, Mike *Sez Who? Sez Me*	E	E	10-12	
Sanders, Thomas E., and Walter W. Peek *Literature of the American Indian*	NF	C	10-12	I
Santoli, Al *Everything We Had: An Oral History of the Vietnam War*	NF	E	9-12	V
Sarton, May *Journal of a Solitude*	NF	E	10-12	
Seki, Joanne Harumi *Being Japanese-American Doesn't Mean Made in Japan*	E	E	9-11	J
Shore, Bradd *Sala'ilua: A Samoan Mystery*	NF	E	10-12	S
Simmen, Edward *Chicano*	E	C	9-12	H

Material	Classification	Type of entry	Grade span	Culture
Steinem, Gloria *Outrageous Acts and Everyday Rebellions*	NF	E	10-12	
Sully, Francois (Ed.) *We the Vietnamese: Voices from Vietnam*	NF	E	9-12	V
Sutter, Frederick *Samoa: A Photographic Essay*	NF	E	9-12	S
Swift, Jonathan *A Modest Proposal*	E	C	10-12	
Syfers, Judy *I Want a Wife*	E	C	10-12	
Tateishi, John *And Justice for All: An Oral History of the Japanese-American Internment Camps*	NF	E	9-12	J
Terkel, Studs *Working*	NF	C	10-12	
Thomas, Lewis *The Medusa and the Snail*	E	C	10-12	
Thoreau, Henry David *Civil Disobedience*	E	C	9-12	
Thoreau, Henry David *Walden*	NF	C	9-12	
Thurber, James *My World and Welcome to It*	E	E	9-12	
Timerman, Jacobo *Prisoner Without a Name, Cell Without a Number*	NF	E	9-12	
Tocqueville, Alexis de *Democracy in America*	E	C	9-12	
Truth, Sojourner "Ain't I a Woman?"	S	C	9-12	B
Twain, Mark Selected essays	E	C	9-12	
Vanzetti, Bartolomeo, and Nicola Sacco *Last Words*	E	E	9-11	

Material	Classifi-cation	Type of entry	Grade span	Culture
Walker, Alice *In Search of Our Mothers' Gardens: Womanist Prose*	E	C	10-12	B
Webb, Sheyann, and Rachel W. Nelson *Selma, Lord, Selma: Girlhood Memories of the Civil-Rights Days*	NF	E	9-12	B
White, E.B. Selected essays	E	C	9-12	
Wollstonecraft, Mary *A Vindication of the Rights of Women*	E	C	10-12	
Woolf, Virginia *A Room of One's Own*	E	C	10-12	
Wright, Richard *White Man, Listen!*	E	C	10-12	B
Yung, Judy, and others (Eds.) *Island: Poetry and History of Chinese Immigrants on Angel Island 1910—1940*	NF	C	9-12	C

Novels

NOVELS encompass an infinite variety of subjects, themes, settings, and moods while illuminating personal, community, and global concerns. At their best, novels teach and inform while entertaining the reader with well-developed characters whose speech and behavior are appropriate to their type, carefully plotted events that are plausible within the context of the story, and a theme or subject area of lasting importance. Young people can come to understand themselves and others a little better through novels, both by validating their own thoughts and feelings as being similar to those experienced by others and by encountering new ideas and situations within a safe environment.

Although the thoughtful reader will gain something from a good novel whether she or he reads it alone or with a group, teacher-guided discussion that includes information on the author and background on the subject can add immeasurably to each student's understanding of the work.

Material	Type of entry	Grade span	Culture
Achebe, Chinua *Things Fall Apart*	E	10-12	B
Agee, James *Death in the Family*	C	10-12	
Anaya, Rudolfo A. *Bless Me, Ultima*	C	10-12	H
Arnow, Harriet *The Dollmaker*	E	10-12	
Austen, Jane *Pride and Prejudice*	C	9-12	
Azuela, Mariano *The Underdogs*	C	9-12	H
Baldwin, James *Go Tell It on the Mountain*	C	10-12	B
Borland, Hal *When the Legends Die*	C	9-11	I

Material	Type of entry	Grade span	Culture
Bradbury, Ray *Fahrenheit 451*	C	9-12	
Bronte, Charlotte *Jane Eyre*	C	9-12	
Bronte, Emily *Wuthering Heights*	C	10-12	
Brookner, Anita *Look at Me*	E	10-12	
Bryant, Dorothy *Miss Giardino*	C	10-12	
Buck, Pearl *The Good Earth*	C	9-11	
Camus, Albert *The Stranger*	C	10-12	
Candelaria, Nash *Memories of the Alhambra*	E	9-12	H
Carroll, Lewis *Alice in Wonderland*	C	9-11	
Cather, Willa *My Antonia*	C	9-12	
Chopin, Kate *The Awakening*	E	11-12	
Cisneros, Sandra *The House on Mango Street*	C	9-12	H
Clark, Walter V. *Ox-Bow Incident*	C	9-11	
Clarke, Arthur C. *Childhood's End*	C	10-12	
Conrad, Joseph *Heart of Darkness*	C	10-12	
Cormier, Robert *The Chocolate War*	C	9-12	

Material	Type of entry	Grade span	Culture
Crane, Stephen *The Red Badge of Courage*	C	9-12	
Craven, Margaret *I Heard the Owl Call My Name*	C	9-11	I
Dickens, Charles *A Tale of Two Cities*	C	9-12	
Doerr, Harriet *Stones for Ibarra*	E	10-12	
Dostoyevsky, Fyodor *Crime and Punishment*	C	10-12	
Ellison, Ralph *Invisible Man*	C	10-12	B
Erdrich, Louise *Love Medicine*	E	10-12	I
Faulkner, William *The Bear*	C	10-12	
Fitzgerald, F. Scott *The Great Gatsby*	C	10-12	
Flaubert, Gustave *Madame Bovary*	C	11-12	
Forbes, Esther *Johnny Tremain*	E	9-10	
Forster, E.M. *A Passage to India*	C	10-12	
Frank, Rudolf *No Hero for the Kaiser*	E	9-11	
Gaines, Ernest J. *The Autobiography of Miss Jane Pittman*	C	9-12	B
Garcia Marquez, Gabriel *Love in the Time of Cholera*	C	11-12	H
Golding, William *Lord of the Flies*	C	9-12	
Green, Hannah *I Never Promised You a Rose Garden*	E	9-11	

Material	Type of entry	Grade span	Culture
Greene, Bette *Summer of My German Soldier*	E	9-11	
Greene, Graham *The Power and the Glory*	C	10-12	
Guest, Judith *Ordinary People*	E	9-12	
Hale, Janet Campbell *The Owl's Song*	E	9-12	I
Hammett, Dashiell *The Maltese Falcon*	E	9-12	
Hardy, Thomas *The Mayor of Casterbridge*	C	10-12	
Hawthorne, Nathaniel *Scarlet Letter*	C	10-12	
Heinlein, Robert A. *Stranger in a Strange Land*	E	10-12	
Heller, Joseph *Catch Twenty-Two*	C	10-12	
Hemingway, Ernest *The Old Man and the Sea*	C	9-12	
Hesse, Hermann *Siddhartha*	C	10-12	
Hinojosa, Rolando *Dear Rafe*	E	9-12	H
Hinton, S.E. *The Outsiders*	C	9-11	
Hugo, Victor *Les Miserables*	C	10-12	
Hurston, Zora Neale *Their Eyes Were Watching God*	C	10-12	B
Huxley, Aldous *Brave New World*	C	10-12	

Material	Type of entry	Grade span	Culture
Islas, Arturo *The Rain God*	E	9-12	H
Jackson, Helen Hunt *Ramona*	E	9-12	I
James, Henry *The Turn of the Screw*	C	10-12	
Jolley, Elizabeth *Miss Peabody's Inheritance*	E	10-12	
Joyce, James *Portrait of the Artist as a Young Man*	C	10-12	
Kawabata, Yasunari *Snow Country*	C	11-12	J
Keyes, Daniel *Flowers for Algernon*	C	9-11	
Kim, Richard E. *Martyred*	C	11-12	K
Kincaid, Jamaica *Annie John*	C	9-11	B
Kinsella, W.P. *Shoeless Joe*	E	10-12	
Knowles, John *Separate Peace*	C	9-11	
LaFarge, Oliver *Laughing Boy*	E	9-12	I
Lawrence, D.H. *Sons and Lovers*	C	10-12	
Lee, Harper *To Kill a Mockingbird*	C	9-11	
Leffland, Ella *Rumors of Peace*	E	10-11	
LeGuin, Ursula K. *The Left Hand of Darkness*	E	9-11	

Material	Type of entry	Grade span	Culture
Lewis, Sinclair *Babbitt*	C	10-12	
Li, Fei-Kan *The Family*	E	10-12	C
Lo, Kuan-Chung *Romance of the Three Kingdoms*	E	10-12	C
London, Jack *Call of the Wild*	C	9-11	
Markandaya, Kamala *Nectar in a Sieve*	E	9-12	
Marshall, Paule *Brown Girl, Brownstones*	C	10-12	B
Mathews, John Joseph *Sundown*	E	9-12	I
Maugham, W. Somerset *Of Human Bondage*	E	10-12	
McCullers, Carson *The Heart Is a Lonely Hunter*	C	9-11	
McCunn, Ruthanne L. *Thousand Pieces of Gold*	E	9-12	C
McKay, Claude *Home to Harlem*	E	10-12	B
Melville, Herman *Billy Budd*	C	10-12	
Mishima, Yukio *The Sound of Waves*	C	10-12	J
Mo, Timothy *Sour Sweet*	C	10-12	C
Momaday, N. Scott *House Made of Dawn*	C	10-12	I
Morrison, Toni *Beloved*	C	10-12	B
Murayama, Milton *All I Asking for Is My Body*	E	9-12	J

Material	Type of entry	Grade span	Culture
Nai-An, Shih *Water Margin*	E	10-12	C
Nordhoff, Charles, and James N. Hall *Mutiny on the Bounty*	E	10-12	
O'Dell, Scott *Sing Down the Moon*	E	10-12	I
Okada, John *No-No Boy*	C	10-12	J
Orwell, George *Animal Farm*	C	9-12	
Paton, Alan *Cry, the Beloved Country*	C	10-12	
Paul, Louis *Pumpkin Coach*	E	9-10	S
Peck, Richard *Remembering the Good Times*	C	9-11	
Peck, Robert Newton *A Day No Pigs Would Die*	C	9-11	
Plath, Sylvia *The Bell Jar*	E	10-12	
Porter, Katherine Anne *Noon Wine*	C	10-12	
Potok, Chaim *Chosen*	C	9-12	
Pym, Barbara *Excellent Women*	E	10-12	
Rawlings, Marjorie K. *The Yearling*	C	9-11	
Remarque, Erich M. *All Quiet on the Western Front*	C	10-12	
Richter, Conrad *Light in the Forest*	C	9-11	

Material	Type of entry	Grade span	Culture
Rivera, Tomás *And the Earth Did Not Part*	C	9-12	H
Ronyoung, Kim *Clay Walls*	C	11-12	K
Saint-Exupery, Antoine de *The Little Prince*	C	9-11	
Salinger, J.D. *The Catcher in the Rye*	C	10-12	
Sandoz, Mari *Cheyenne Autumn*	E	9-12	I
Saroyan, William *The Human Comedy*	C	9-11	
Schaefer, Jack *Shane*	E	9-11	
Scott, Sir Walter *Ivanhoe*	E	9-11	
Shirota, Jon *Lucky Come Hawaii*	E	10-12	J
Silko, Leslie Marmon *Ceremony*	E	10-12	I
Solzhenitsyn, Alexander *One Day in the Life of Ivan Denisovich*	C	10-12	
Steinbeck, John *Of Mice and Men*	C	9-12	
Stevenson, Robert Louis *Strange Case of Dr. Jekyll and Mr. Hyde*	E	9-11	
Swift, Jonathan *Gulliver's Travels*	C	10-12	
Tanizaki, Junichiro *Some Prefer Nettles*	E	10-12	J
Theroux, Paul *The Mosquito Coast*	E	10-12	

Material	Type of entry	Grade span	Culture
Tolkien, J.R.R. *The Hobbit*	E	9-12	
Tolstoy, Leo *Anna Karenina*	C	11-12	
Trollope, Anthony *Barchester Towers*	C	11-12	
Twain, Mark *The Adventures of Huckleberry Finn*	C	9-12	
Tyler, Anne *The Tin Can Tree*	E	10-12	
Uchida, Yoshiko *Picture Bride*	C	9-12	J
Updike, John *Centaur*	C	10-12	
Vargas-Llosa, Mario *Aunt Julia and the Scriptwriter*	E	9-12	H
Villarreal, Jose A. *Pocho*	E	10-12	H
Vonnegut, Kurt, Jr. *Cat's Cradle*	E	10-12	
Watkins, Yoko K. *So Far from the Bamboo Grove*	E	9-12	J
Welch, James *The Death of Jim Loney*	E	10-12	I
Weldon, Fay *Letters to Alice: On First Reading Jane Austen*	E	10-12	
Wells, H.G. *War of the Worlds*	E	9-12	
Wharton, Edith *Ethan Frome*	C	10-12	
Wright, Richard *Native Son*	C	10-12	B
Zindel, Paul *The Pigman*	C	9-11	

Poetry

THROUGHOUT the ages poetry has brought delight, afforded comfort, and presented new patterns for looking at everyday occurrences. Poets create moods and images through their economy of language, their talent for choosing the perfect word tuned to the mood of the moment, and their perceptive, intimate responses to universal emotions. With its inner melody, rhythm, repetition of sound patterns, intensity of emotion, and its rich use of metaphor, most poetry sings when it is read aloud. Poetry is tailored to the tongue; and because of this oral/aural quality, it is ideal for the classroom. When a poem is read aloud, every student experiences it for that moment. The true appreciation of the poem may occur later, much later, for as Robert Frost once said, "A poem begins in delight and ends in wisdom."

It is hoped that the delight will come from the variety of poetry offered within this list of suggested readings. The poets included are representative of many forms of poetry: narrative, lyric, ballad, and free verse. The ethnic and cultural voices and styles of many people are reflected. Both classic and contemporary poets have been selected so that students will discover that poetry is very much alive and that there is always space for a personal interpretation of a well-known poem. Perhaps students will feel as the natives of Kenya felt when the novelist Isak Dinesen recited English poetry to them. They understood nothing but begged her to recite the poems again and again, or, in their words, *to speak like rain*. Perhaps students will carry this a step further and be motivated to find their own favorite poet whose voice truly speaks to them.

The following list of specific poems is intended simply to give teachers suggestions of where to begin with a particular poet with whom the teacher may be unfamiliar or to suggest a new poem by a familiar poet. Clearly, there is no single poem that is representative of any poet just as there is no single poem that is an appropriate selection for all students. The members of the committee hope that these selections will be useful in introducing students to a wide range of poems and poets.

Material	Type of entry	Grade span	Culture
Poems by Individual Poets			
Allen, Paula Gunn "Grandmother"	C	9-11	I
Arnold, Matthew "Dover Beach"	C	10-12	
Ashbery, John "Rivers and Mountains"	E	10-12	
Auden, W.H. "Musée des Beaux Arts"	C	9-12	
Barker, George "Sonnet to My Mother"	C	9-12	
Berry, Wendell "Independence Day"	C	9-12	
Berryman, John "Henry's Confession"	E	10-12	
Bishop, Elizabeth "One Art"	C	9-12	
Blake, William "The Tyger"	C	9-12	
Bly, Robert "Watching Television"	C	9-12	
Bogan, Louise "Medusa"	E	9-12	
Borges, Jorge Luis "Things That Might Have Been"	E	10-12	
Brooke, Rupert "The Soldier"	C	9-12	
Brooks, Gwendolyn "The Bean Eaters"	C	9-12	B
Browning, Elizabeth Barrett "How Do I Love Thee? Let Me Count the Ways"	C	9-12	
Browning, Robert "My Last Duchess"	C	9-12	

Material	Type of entry	Grade span	Culture
Bryant, William Cullen "Thanatopsis"	C	9-12	
Byron, George G., Lord "She Walks in Beauty"	C	10-12	
Castillo, Ana "Napa, California"	E	9-11	H
Cavafy, Constantine "The Mirror in the Front Hall"	C	9-12	
Cervantes, Lorna Dee "Beneath the Shadow of the Freeway"	E	9-11	H
Chang, Diana "The Horizon Is Definitely Speaking"	E	10-12	C
Chaucer, Geoffrey "The Prologue to the Canterbury Tales"	C	9-12	
Coleridge, Samuel Taylor "Kubla Khan; or, A Vision in a Dream"	C	10-11	
Conjugacion, Noland "Coconut Girl"	C	10-12	F
Crane, Hart "My Grandmother's Love Letters"	C	9-12	
Cullen, Countee "Incident"	C	9-12	B
Cummings, E.E. "In Just-Spring"	C	9-12	
Dickey, James "The Heaven of Animals"	C	9-12	
Dickey, William "Tutankhamen"	C	9-12	
Dickinson, Emily "After Great Pain a Formal Feeling Comes"	C	9-12	
Donne, John "Sonnet 10: Death Be Not Proud, Though Some Have Called Thee"	C	9-12	

Material	Type of entry	Grade span	Culture
Doolittle, Hilda "Orchard"	E	9-12	
Dunbar, Paul L. "Sympathy"	C	9-12	B
Duncan, Robert "My Mother Would Be a Falconress"	E	10-12	
Eberhart, Richard "The Groundhog"	C	9-12	
Eliot, T.S. "The Love Song of J. Alfred Prufrock"	C	9-12	
Evans, Mari "When in Rome"	E	9-11	
Ferlinghetti, Lawrence "Constantly Risking Absurdity"	E	9-12	
Field, Edward "Icarus"	C	9-12	
Francis, Robert "The Base Stealer"	C	9-12	
Frost, Robert "The Road Not Taken"	C	9-12	
García Lorca, Federico "Guitar"	E	10-12	H
Giovanni, Nikki "The Funeral of Martin Luther King, Jr."	E	9-12	B
Gunn, Thom "St. Martin and the Beggar"	C	10-12	
Hall, Donald "The Child"	C	9-12	
Hardy, Thomas "The Darkling Thrush"	C	10-12	
Hayden, Robert "Those Winter Sundays"	C	9-12	B

Material	Type of entry	Grade span	Culture
Homer "The Odyssey"	C	9-12	
Hongo, Garrett Kaoru "Yellow Light"	C	9-12	J
Hopkins, Gerard Manley "God's Grandeur"	C	10-12	
Housman, A.E. "To an Athlete Dying Young"	C	9-12	
Hughes, Langston "Dream Deferred"	C	9-12	B
Hughes, Ted "Hawk Roosting"	C	9-12	
Huynh, Sanh Thong "Tale of Kieu"	C	9-12	V
Jarrell, Randall "The Death of the Ball Turret Gunner"	C	9-12	
Jeffers, Robinson "Hurt Hawks"	C	9-12	
Johnson, James Weldon "The Creation"	E	9-12	B
Jordan, June "If You Saw a Negro Lady"	E	9-12	B
Justice, Donald "Poem to Be Read at 3 A.M."	C	9-12	
Keats, John "Ode on a Grecian Urn"	C	9-12	
Kimura, Audy "Lovers and Friends"	C	10-12	J
Kinnell, Galway "The Bear"	C	10-12	
Kizer, Carolyn "The Great Blue Heron"	C	10-12	

Material	Type of entry	Grade span	Culture
Kumin, Maxine "For a Shetland Pony Brood Mare Who Died in Her Barren Year"	C	9-12	
Larkin, Philip "Toads"	E	9-12	
Levertov, Denise "The Springtime"	E	9-12	
Levine, Philip "The Horse"	E	9-12	
Lowell, Amy "Patterns"	C	9-12	
Lowell, Robert "Mr. Edwards and the Spider"	E	10-12	
MacLeish, Archibald "Ars Poetica"	C	9-12	
Marcus, Adrianne "Child of Earthquake Country"	E	10-12	
Marvell, Andrew "To His Coy Mistress"	E	10-12	
McKay, Claude "The Tropics in New York"	E	9-12	B
Meredith, William "The Open Sea"	C	9-12	
Merwin, W.S. "For the Anniversary of My Death"	C	10-12	
Miles, Josephine "Memorial Day"	C	9-12	
Millay, Edna St. Vincent "Dirge Without Music"	C	9-12	
Milton, John "On His Blindness"	C	10-12	
Mohr, Nicholasa "Nilda"	C	9-12	H
Moore, Marianne "Poetry"	C	9-12	

Material	Type of entry	Grade span	Culture
Morgan, Edwin "Strawberries"	E	9-12	
Nemerov, Howard "The Town Dump"	E	9-12	
Neruda, Pablo "Our Child"	E	10-12	H
Olson, Charles "Maximus, to Himself"	E	10-12	
Ortiz, Simon "My Father's Song"	E	9-12	I
Owen, Wilfred "Dulce et decorum est"	C	10-12	
Pastan, Linda "Grammar Lesson"	E	9-12	
Paulzine, Niki "I Am the Fire of Time"	E	9-12	I
Pavese, Cesare "Ulysses"	C	10-12	H
Piercy, Marge "For the Young Who Want To"	C	9-12	
Plath, Sylvia "Daddy"	E	10-12	
Pound, Ezra "The River Merchant's Wife: A Letter"	C	10-12	
Reed, Henry "The Naming of Parts"	C	9-12	
Reed, Ishmael "Beware: Do Not Read This Poem"	C	9-12	B
Rich, Adrienne "Diving into the Wreck"	C	9-12	
Robinson, Edwin A. "Richard Cory"	C	9-12	
Roethke, Theodore "My Papa's Waltz"	C	9-12	

Material	Type of entry	Grade span	Culture
Rose, Wendy "I Expected My Skin and My Blood to Ripen"	C	9-12	I
Rukeyser, Muriel "The Question"	C	9-12	
Sandburg, Carl "Fog"	C	9-12	
Sappho "My Mother Always Said"	C	10-12	
Sexton, Anne "Unknown Girl in the Maternity Ward"	E	10-12	
Shapiro, Karl "Auto Wreck"	C	9-12	
Shelley, Percy Bysshe "Ozymandias"	C	9-12	
Simic, Charles "Sleep"	E	10-12	
Simpson, Louis "My Father in the Night Commanding No"	E	10-12	
Snyder, Gary "Hay for the Horses"	C	9-12	
So, Chongju "Unforgettable Things"	C	9-12	K
Spender, Stephen "I Think Continually of Those Who Were Truly Great"	C	10-12	
Stafford, William "Traveling Through the Dark"	C	9-12	
Stevens, Wallace "Thirteen Ways of Looking at a Blackbird"	C	9-12	
Swenson, May "Southbound on the Freeway"	C	9-11	
Teasdale, Sara "Barter"	E	9-12	
Tennyson, Alfred "Ulysses"	C	9-12	

Material	Type of entry	Grade span	Culture
Thomas, Dylan "Do Not Go Gentle into That Good Night"	C	9-12	
Voznesensky, Andrei "Dead Still"	C	9-12	
Wakoski, Diane "Justice Is Reason Enough"	E	9-12	
Walters, Anna Lee "A Teacher Taught Me"	E	9-12	B
Warren, Robert Penn "Letter from a Coward to a Hero"	C	10-12	
Watkins, Vernon "The Heron"	E	9-12	
Wendt, Albert "What Do You Do Now Brother?"	C	10-12	S
Whitman, Walt "I Hear America Singing"	C	9-12	
Wilbur, Richard "Mind"	E	9-12	
Williams, William Carlos "This Is Just to Say"	C	9-12	
Wilson, Ramona C. "Keeping Hair"	E	9-11	I
Wordsworth, William "I Wandered Lonely as a Cloud"	C	9-12	
Wright, James "A Blessing"	C	10-12	
Wylie, Elinor "Velvet Shoes"	E	9-11	
Yeats, William Butler "The Second Coming"	C	9-12	
Yevtushenko, Yevgeny "People"	C	9-12	

Material	Culture
Poetry Collections	
Adoff, Arnold (Ed.) *Celebrations: A New Anthology of Black American Poetry*	B
Balaban, John (Ed.) *Vietnamese Folk Poetry*	V
Basho, Matsuo *Seven Poems*	J
Bay Area Filipino Writers *Without Names: A Collection of Poems*	F
Bierhorst, John (Ed.) *In the Trail of the Wind: American Indian Poems and Ritual Orations*	I
Bontemps, Arna (Ed.) *American Negro Poetry*	B
Chin, Marilyn *Dwarf Bamboo*	Kh
Fisher, Dexter (Ed.) *Third Woman: Minority Woman Writers of the United States*	I
Fleischman, Paul *A Joyful Noise*	
Gould, Jean (Ed.) *American Women Poets*	
Hiura, Jerrold A. *Hawk's Well: A Collection of Japanese-American Art and Literature*	J

Material	Culture
Hobson, Geary (Ed.) *Remembered Earth: An Anthology of Contemporary Native American Literature*	I
Hongo, Garrett Kaoru *River of Heaven*	J
Huynh, Sanh Thong (Ed.) *The Heritage Vietnamese Poetry*	V
Janeczko, Paul B. (Ed.) *Poetspeak: In Their Work, About Their Work*	
Jimenez, Juan R. *Platero and I*	H
Kanellos, Nicolas (Ed.) *Decade of Hispanic Literature: An Anniversary Anthology*	H
Kemp, Milos *Aztec Poems*	I
Kim, Joyce Jarhyun *Master Poems of Modern Korea Since 1920: An Anthology of Modern Korean Poetry*	K
Kim, Jungshik *Lost Love: 99 Poems*	K
Kim, Yeol-kyu *Korean Poetry*	K
Kissam, Edward, and Michael Schmidt (Eds.) *Poems of the Aztec Peoples*	H/I

Material	Culture
Lau, Alan C. *Songs for Jadina*	Kh
Lee, Peter H. *Poems from Korea*	K
Lewis, Richard (Ed.) *I Breathe a New Song: Poems of the Eskimo*	I
Livingston, Myra C. (Ed.) *Why Am I Grown So Cold: Poems of the Unknowable*	
Lomax, Alan, and Raoul Abdul (Eds.) *Three-Thousand Years of Black Poetry: An Anthology*	B
Lueders, Edward, and Primus St. John (Eds.) *Zero Makes Me Hungry: A Collection of Poems for Today*	
Lum, Wing Tek *Expounding the Doubtful Points*	Kh
Masters, Edgar Lee *Spoon River Anthology*	
McCullough, Frances (Ed.) *Love Is Like the Lion's Tooth*	
Niatum, Duane (Ed.) *Harper's Anthology of Twentieth Century Native American Poetry*	I
Okubo, Mine *Citizen 13660*	J

Material	Culture
Paz, Octavio (Ed.) *Anthology of Mexican Poetry*	H
Pietri, Pedro *Traffic Violations*	H
Plotz, Helen (Ed.) *Imagination's Other Place: Poems of Science and Mathematics*	
Randall, Dudley (Ed.) *Black Poets*	B
Rose, Wendy *Hopi Roadrunner, Dancing*	I
Rothenberg, Jerome (Ed.) *Shaking the Pumpkin: Traditional Poetry of the Indian North Americas*	I
Shakespeare, William *Sonnets*	
Song, Cathy *Picture Bride*	Kh
Steiner, Stan, and Luis Valdez (Eds.) *Aztlan: An Anthology of Mexican-American Literature*	H
Vigil, Evangelina (Ed.) *Woman of Her Word: Hispanic Women Write*	H
Yamada, Mitsuye *Camp Notes and Other Poems*	J

Short Stories

*T*HE short story is one type of literature that can serve as a mirror in which the reader can see and understand himself or herself. In a brief fictional prose narrative, the author creates a unified impression quickly and forcefully. The modern short story often uses unresolved situations instead of the more familiar narrative pattern of resolution of the action. The history of the short story can trace its beginning to biblical stories such as that of David and Goliath.

Material	Type of entry	Grade span	Culture
Akutagawa, Ryunosuke "Rashomon"	E	10-12	J
Asimov, Isaac "Ugly Little Boy"	E	9-12	
Bambara, Toni C. "Blues Ain't No Mockin' Bird"	E	10-12	B
Barthelme, Donald "Indian Uprising"	C	10-12	
Berriault, Gina "Stone Boy"	C	9-11	
Bierce, Ambrose "Occurrence at Owl Creek Bridge"	C	10-12	
Bradbury, Ray "All Summer in a Day"	E	9-12	
Cameron, Peter "Homework"	C	10-12	
Campbell, Janet "Snow Keeps Falling"	E	9-11	I
Capote, Truman "Christmas Memory"	C	9-12	
Cather, Willa "Paul's Case"	C	10-12	

Material	Type of entry	Grade span	Culture
Chan, Jeffery, and others (Eds.) "Aiiieeeee!"	C	10-12	C/F/J
Cheever, John "The Swimmer"	E	10-12	
Chekhov, Anton P. "The Bet"	C	10-12	
Chin, Frank "Food for All His Dead"	E	10-12	C
Chock, Eric, and Darrell Lum (Eds.) "The Best of Bamboo Ridge"	C	9-12	Hm
Chopin, Kate "Story of an Hour"	C	10-12	
Colette "Little Bouillouix Girl"	E	10-12	
Connell, Richard "Most Dangerous Game"	C	9-11	
Cormier, Robert "Eight Plus One"	E	9-11	
Crane, Stephen "Open Boat"	C	10-12	
Faulkner, William "Barn Burning"	C	9-12	
Fisher, Dorothy Canfield "Bedquilt"	E	9-11	
Freeman, Mary W. "Revolt of 'Mother'"	C	9-11	
Galsworthy, John "Apple Tree"	C	10-12	
Garland, Hamlin "Under the Lion's Paw"	C	9-12	
Gilchrist, Ellen "Victory Over Japan"	E	10-12	
Gilman, Charlotte P. "Yellow Wallpaper"	C	10-12	

Material	Type of entry	Grade span	Culture
Gogol, Nikolai "The Overcoat"	C	10-12	
Gordimer, Nadine "My First Two Women"	C	10-12	
Greene, Graham "The Destructors"	C	9-11	
Harte, Bret "Outcasts of Poker Flat"	C	9-11	
Hawthorne, Nathaniel "Young Goodman Brown"	C	10-12	
Hemingway, Ernest "Snows of Kilimanjaro"	C	10-12	
Hempel, Amy "In the Cemetery Where Al Jolson Is Buried"	C	10-12	
Henry, O. "The Gift of the Magi"	E	9-11	
Houston, James "Gasoline"	E	10-12	
Hurst, James "Scarlet Ibis: A Classic Story of Brotherhood"	C	9-11	
Hwang, Sun-won "Cranes" in *Flowers of Fire: Twentieth-Century Korean Stories*. Edited by Peter H. Lee	C	9-12	K
Irving, Washington "The Devil and Tom Walker"	C	9-12	
Jackson, Shirley "The Lottery"	C	10-12	
Jacobs, W.W. "Monkey's Paw"	C	9-12	
Jewett, Sarah Orne "A White Heron"	E	9-12	
Johnson, Dorothy M. "The Hanging Tree"	E	9-12	

Material	Type of entry	Grade span	Culture
Joyce, James "Dubliners"	C	10-12	
Kafka, Franz "The Metamorphosis"	C	10-12	
Kang, Sinjae "Young Zelkova" in *Flowers of Fire: Twentieth-Century Korean Stories.* Edited by Peter H. Lee	C	9-12	K
Kelly, William D. "Visit to Grandmother"	E	9-11	B
Kim, Tongni "Portrait of Shaman" in *Flowers of Fire: Twentieth-Century Korean Stories.* Edited by Peter H. Lee	C	9-12	K
Lawrence, D. H. "The Rocking Horse Winner"	C	10-12	
Laygo, Terisita M. "The Well of Time"	C	9-12	F
Lessing, Doris "The Old Woman and Her Cat"	E	9-12	
Malamud, Bernard "Summer's Reading"	E	9-12	
Mansfield, Katherine "Her First Ball"	C	10-12	
Maugham, W. Somerset "Verger"	C	10-12	
Maupassant, Guy de "The Necklace"	C	9-11	
Mori, Toshio "Yokohama, California"	C	9-12	J
Munro, H.H. (Saki) "Open Window"	C	10-12	
Oates, Joyce Carol "Where Are You Going, Where Have You Been?"	E	10-12	
O'Conner, Flannery "Confession"	C	10-12	

Material	Type of entry	Grade span	Culture
Oe, Kenzaburo (Ed.) "The Crazy Iris"	E	10-12	J
O'Flaherty, Liam "The Test of Courage and All Things Come of Age"	C	9-11	
Paley, Grace "Samuel"	C	10-12	
Parker, Dorothy "Arrangement in Black and White"	C	10-12	
Poe, Edgar Allan "The Cask of Amontillado"	C	9-11	
Porter, Katherine Anne "The Jilting of Granny Weatherall"	C	10-12	
Powers, J.F. "Valiant Woman"	C	10-12	
Rulfo, Juan "We're Very Poor"	C	9-12	H
Salinger, J.D. "For Esme, with Love and Squalor"	C	10-12	
Santos, Bienvenido N. "Scent of Apples"	C	9-12	F
Shaw, Irwin "Pattern of Love"	E	9-12	
Singer, Isaac Bashevis "Yentl the Yeshiva Boy"	E	9-12	
Stafford, Jean "Bad Characters"	C	10-12	
Steinbeck, John "Flight"	C	9-12	
Stuart, Jesse "Split Cherry Tree"	C	9-12	
Sunu, Hwi "Flowers of Fire" in *Flowers of Fire: Twentieth-Century Korean Stories.* Edited by Peter H. Lee	C	9-12	K

Material	Type of entry	Grade span	Culture
Tagatac, Samuel "New Anak"	C	10-12	F
Thomas, Dylan "A Child's Christmas in Wales"	C	9-12	
Thurber, James "The Secret Life of Walter Mitty"	C	9-12	
Tolstoy, Leo "How Much Land Does a Man Need?"	C	9-12	
Trilling, Lionel "Of This Time, of That Place"	C	10-12	
Twain, Mark "Celebrated Jumping Frog of Calaveras County"	C	9-11	
Vandervelde, Marjorie "Across the Tundra"	C	9-10	I
Vonnegut, Kurt, Jr. "Harrison Bergeron"	C	10-12	
Waugh, Evelyn "Mr. Loveday's Little Outing"	C	10-12	
Welty, Eudora "The Worn Path"	C	9-12	B
West, Jessamyn "Condemned Librarian"	C	10-12	
Williams, William Carlos "Use of Force"	C	10-12	
Wong, Shawn "Each Year Grain"	C	10-12	C
Wright, Richard "The Man Who Went to College"	C	10-12	B
Yamamoto, Hisaye "Las Vegas Charley"	E	10-12	J
Yi, Hoesong "Woman Who Fulled Clothes" in *Flowers of Fire: Twentieth-Century Korean Stories*. Edited by Peter H. Lee	C	9-12	K
Yi, Hyosok "Buckwheat Season" in *Flowers of Fire: Twentieth-Century Korean Stories*. Edited by Peter H. Lee	C	9-12	K

Books in Languages Other Than English

BOOKS that are written in languages other than English are suggested for students who read in another language better than they can in English. The books are acknowledged literature of merit chosen by teachers and other educators who have relied on them to teach literature to students who have yet to learn how to read English. As these non-English-reading students quickly learn to read in English, they are exposed to the books on the other lists.

This category could include books from many languages; however, several factors mitigate against listing them all. Therefore, we have limited our entries to those in Chinese, Hmong, Japanese, Khmer, Korean, Pilipino, Samoan, Spanish, and Vietnamese.

The matrix for this category gives the user the following information:

Column 1 shows the language in which the book is written; for example:

C—Chinese   P—Pilipino
Hm—Hmong   Sam—Samoan
J—Japanese   S—Spanish
K—Korean   V—Vietnamese
Kh—Khmer

Column 2 indicates the type of literature; for example:

B—Biography   N—Novel
D—Drama   NF—Nonfiction
E—Essay   PA—Poetry anthology
F—Folklore   PI—Individual poet
FE—Folklore epic   SS—Short story
FM—Folklore mythology

Column 3 indicates whether the material is core (C), extended (E), or recreational/motivational (R/M).

Column 4 shows the suggested grade span.

Material	Language	Type of literature	Type of entry	Grade span
Aesop *Aesop's Fables*	C	F	C	9-12
Alcott, Louisa May *Little Women*	C	N	C	9-10
Alcott, Louisa May *Mujercitas (Little Women)*	S	N	C	9-10
Anonymous *Cantar de mío cid (El Cid)*	S	FE	E	9-12
Anonymous *Chunhyangjon*	K	N	C	9-12
Anonymous *Ise Tale: Azuma kudari, azusa yumi*	J	PA	C	9-10
Anonymous *Kokin' shuu Tale and Others: Oochoo no uta*	J	PA	C	9-10
Anonymous *Three-Hundred Tang Poems* (Annotated)	C	PA	E	9-12
Anonymous *Ujishuui Tale: Inaka no ko*	J	FM	C	9-10
Anonymous *Yamato Tale: Ubasute*	J	FM	C	9-10
Arevalo-Martínez, Rafael *Los hombres-lobos*	S	PI	C	9-12
Arrcola, Juan José *El guardagujas*	S	SS	E	9-12
Barrett, Joseph H. *The Life of Abraham Lincoln*	C	B	C	11-12
Borges, Jorge L. *El sur (The South)*	S	SS	R/M	9-12
Bronte, Emily *Wuthering Heights*	C	N	C	11-12
Bronte, Emily *Cumbres, borrascosas (Wuthering Heights)*	S	N	C	11-12
Buck, Pearl S. *La buena tierra (The Good Earth)*	S	N	E	9-12

Material	Language	Type of literature	Type of entry	Grade span
Bulosan, Carlos, Jr. *The Philippines Is in the Heart: A Collection of Short Stories*	P	SS	E	9-10
Camus, Albert *El extranjero (The Stranger)*	S	SS	C	10-12
Cervantes, Miguel de *Don Quijote de la Mancha*	S	N	C	11-12
Chae, Man-Shik *Selected Works of Chae, Man-Shik*	K	SS	E	9-12
Chen, Jack (Chen Yi-fan) *The Chinese of America*	C	NF	C	9-12
Chen, Jo-hsi (Chen Ruo-xi) *The Execution of Mayor Yin*	C	SS	E	11-12
Conrad, Joseph *Lord Jim*	S	N	E	9-12
Cortazar, Julio *El axolotl (The Amphibian)*	S	SS	R/M	9-12
Cruz, Juana Inés de la *Arguye de inconsecuencia el gusto y la censura de los hombres, que en las mujeres acusan lo que causan (Against the Inconsequence of Men's Desires and Their Censure of Women for Faults Which They Themselves Have Caused)*	S	PI	R/M	9-12
Cuu Long Giang-Toan Anh *Nguoi viet dat viet (Vietnam People and Land)*	V	NF	E	9-12
DaCal, Ernesto G., and Margarita Ucelay *Literatura del siglo XX*	S	PA	E	9-12
Dao, Dang Vy *Nguyen tri phuong, nhat gia tam kiet (The Three Heroes in One Family)*	V	B	E	9-12
Darío, Rubén *Sonatina*	S	PI	E	9-12
Defoe, Daniel *Robinson Crusoe*	S	N	E	9-12
Dickens, Charles *La historia de dos ciudades (A Tale of Two Cities)*	S	N	C	9-10

Material	Language	Type of literature	Type of entry	Grade span
Dickens, Charles *A Tale of Two Cities*	C	N	C	9-10
Doan, Quoc Sy *Ba sinh huong lua (Keep the Fire Glow Forever)*	V	F	R/M	9-12
Dostoyevsky, Fyodor *Crimen y castigo (Crime and Punishment)*	S	N	C	10-12
Dumas, Alexandre *The Count of Monte Cristo*	C	N	C	9-10
Dumas, Alexandre *El Conde de Monte Cristo (The Count of Monte Cristo)*	S	N	C	9-10
Duong Quang Ham *Viet Nam thi van hop tuyen (Selected Vietnamese Literature)*	V	PA	C	9-12
Enríquez, Mig A. *Three Philippines Epic Plays*	P	D	R/M	9-10
Enríquez, Salud, and others *Kariktan: Mga kuwentong walang kupas (The World's Best Loved Stories)*	P	SS	E	9-10
Espronceda, José de *Canción del pirata*	S	PI	E	9-12
Fernández de Lizardi, José J. *El periquillo sarniento (The Itching Parrot)*	S	N	E	9-12
Frank, Anne *Diario de Ana Frank (The Diary of Anne Frank)*	S	B	C	9-12
Franklin, Benjamin *The Autobiography of Benjamin Franklin*	C	B	C	9-10
García Lorca, Federico *Lament for the Death of a Bullfighter*	S	PI	C	9-12
Golding, William *El amo de las moscas (Lord of the Flies)* (Translated by W. Solden)	S	N	C	9-12
Guiraldes, Ricardo *Don segundo sombra*	S	N	E	9-12
Ha, Mai Anh *Vo gia dinh* (A translation of *Sans famille* by Hector Marlot)	V	F	E	9-12

Material	Language	Type of literature	Type of entry	Grade span
Hagiwara, Asataroo *Take; Chuugaku no kootei*	J	PI	C	11-12
Han Mac Tu *Tho (Poems)*	V	PI	C	9-12
Hemingway, Ernest *Por quien dobla la campana (For Whom the Bell Tolls)*	S	N	C	10-12
Hernández, José *El Gaucho Martín Fierro*	S	F	C	9-12
Hoa Bang *Quang trung nguyen hue*	V	B	C	9-12
Hoai Thanh, Hoai Chan *Thi nhan Viet Nam (The Vietnamese Poets)*	V	B	C	9-12
Hoang, Trong Mien *Viet Nam van hoc toan thu (Vietnamese Literature),* Volume 1	V	FM	C	9-12
Hoang, Trong Mien *Viet Nam van hoc toan thu (Vietnamese Literature),* Volume 2	V	F	C	9-12
Huffman, Franklin E., and Im Proum *Cambodian Literary Reader and Glossary*	Kh	NF	C	9-12
Huffman, Franklin E., and Im Proum *Cambodian Reader (Intermediate)*	Kh	NF	C	9-12
Huy Can *Lua thieng (The Sacred Fire)*	V	PI	C	9-12
Hyon, Jin-Kon *Selected Works of Hyon, Jin-Kon*	K	SS	E	9-12
Ibsen, Henrik *Casa de muñecas (A Doll's House)*	S	F	C	9-12
Isaacs, Jorge *Maria: A South American Romance*	S	N	R/M	9-12
Jin, Ba *Spring*	C	N	E	9-12
Johnson, Charles (Ed.) *Dab neeg hmoob*	Hm	F	R/M	9-10
Kamono, Choumei *Hoojooki: Yuku kawa no nagare*	J	E	C	9-10

Material	Language	Type of literature	Type of entry	Grade span
Kato, Shuuton *Haiku en'kin*	J	PA	C	9-10
Keller, Helen *La historia de mi vida (The Story of My Life)*	S	B	C	9-10
Keller, Helen *The Story of My Life*	C	B	C	9-10
Kim, Dong-Ni *Selected Works of Kim, Dong-Ni*	K	SS	E	9-12
King Ang Duong Kakei *The Story of Dame Kakei*	Kh	PI	C	10-12
Lamb, Charles, and Mary Lamb *Tales from Shakespeare*	C	D	C	9-10
Lao She *The Teahouse*	C	D	E	11-12
Laygo, Teresita *The Well of Time: Eighteen Short Stories from Philippine Contemporary Literature*	P	SS	C	9-10
Lee, Kwang-Soo *Selected Works of Lee, Kwang-Soo*	K	N	E	9-12
Le Ngo Cat and Pham, Dinh To *Dai nam quoc su dien ca (The History of Dai Nam in Verse)*	V	PA	C	9-12
Le Van Sieu *Van minh Vietnam (The Civilization of Vietnam)*	V	NF	C	9-12
Llewellyn, Richard *Qué verde era mi valle (How Green Was My Valley)*	S	N	C	9-10
López y Fuentes, Gregorio *Una carta a Dios (A Letter to God)*	S	SS	E	9-12
Luo Guan-Zhong *Romance of the Three Kingdoms*	C	N	R/M	11-12
Luu, Trong Lu *Tieng thu (The Sound of Autumn)*	V	PI	C	9-12
Lu Xun *Cry*	C	SS	C	11-12
Machado, Antonio *Caminos (Roads)*	S	PI	E	9-12

Material	Language	Type of literature	Type of entry	Grade span
Manrique, Jorge *Coplas que hizo por la muerte de su padre*	S	PI	E	9-12
Marques, René *La carreta (The Cart)*	S	D	E	9-12
Martí, Jose *Versos sencillos (Simple Verses)*	S	PI	C	9-12
McCullers, Carson *El corazón es un cazador solitario (The Heart Is a Lonely Hunter)*	S	N	C	9-12
Melville, Herman *Moby Dick*	C	N	C	10-12
Miller, Arthur *La muerte de un vendedor (The Death of a Salesman)*	S	D	C	10-12
Mistral, Gabriela *Desolación*	S	PI	E	9-12
Mistral, Gabriela *La maestra rural (The Rural Schoolteacher)*	S	PI	C	9-12
Miyoshi, Tatsuji *Kame no ue* (and others)	J	PI	C	9-10
Moyle, Richard *Fagogo*	Sam	F	C	10-12
Mu Ling Qi (Ed.) *Selected Essays by Overseas Chinese Writers*	C	E	E	9-12
Murou, Suisei *Sabishiki haru* (and others)	J	PI	C	9-10
Nakajima, Atsushi *Sangetsu ki*	J	N	C	11-12
Nervo, Amado *En paz (In Peace)*	S	PI	C	9-12
Nguyen, Khac Ngu *My thuat co truyen Viet Nam (The Traditional Fine Arts of Vietnam)*	V	NF	E	9-12
Nguyen, Lang *Van lang di su (The Extraordinary History of Van Lang)*	V	FM	C	9-12

Material	Language	Type of literature	Type of entry	Grade span
Nguyen, True Phuong *Van hoc binh dan*	V	NF	C	9-12
Nguyen, Tu Nang *Than thoai Vietnam (The Mythologies of Vietnam)*	V	FM	C	9-12
Nguyen, Van Ngoc *Truyen co nuoc nam (Legends of Vietnam,* Volume I, *People)*	V	F	R/M	9-12
Nhok, Them *Kolap peilin (The Rose of Peilin)*	Kh	N	C	10-12
Nhuong Tong *Nguyen thai hoc*	V	B	C	9-12
Nou, Hach *Phka srapone (The Wilted Flower)*	Kh	N	C	10-12
Ogawa, Kunio *Yoru no suiei*	J	N	C	9-10
Oono, Yasaumaro *Kojiki; Taka ikuya*	J	PA	C	11-12
Ootomono, Yakamochi *Man'yooshuu*	J	PA	C	11-12
Ortega y Gasset, José *La rebelión de las masas*	S	E	E	11-12
Ouk Mory *Cambodian Primer*	Kh	SS	C	9-10
Paz, Octavio *Máscaras mexicanas (Mexican Masks)*	S	E	C	9-12
Pérez-Galdós, Benito *Marianela*	S	N	E	9-12
Phan Nhat Nam *Mua he do lua (Summer of Glowing Fire)*	V	E	E	9-12
Preah Padumatther Som *The Story of Tum Teav*	Kh	PI	C	10-12
Quiroga, Horacio *El desierto*	S	SS	E	9-12
Rivera, Tomás *Y no se lo tragó la tierra (And the Earth Did Not Part)*	S	N	R/M	9-12

Material	Language	Type of literature	Type of entry	Grade span
Rizal, José *El filibusterismo (The Reign of Greed)*	P	N	C	9-12
Rizal, José *Noli me tángere (Social Cancer)*	P	N	C	9-12
Rulfo, Juan *Es que somos pobres (We're Very Poor)*	S	SS	C	9-12
St. John of the Cross *La noche oscura del alma (The Dark Night of the Soul)*	S	PI	C	9-12
Sánchez Mejías, Ignacio *Elegy on the Death of the Famed Bullfighter*	S	PI	E	9-12
Santos, Bienvenido N. *The Day the Dancers Came*	P	SS	R/M	9-10
Seishoo, Nagon *Makura no sooshi: Haru wa akebono*	J	E	C	11-12
Selected Vietnamese Writers *Nhung truyen ngan hay nhat cua que huong chung ta (The Most Interesting Short Stories of Our Homeland)*	V	SS	E	9-12
Shakespeare, William *King Lear*	C	D	C	11-12
Shakespeare, William *The Tragedy of Hamlet*	C	D	C	9-12
Shakespeare, William *The Tragedy of Macbeth*	C	D	C	11-12
Shen Cong-wen (Shen Ts'ung-wen) *Border Town*	C	N	E	11-12
Shi Nai-an *Outlaws of the Marches (or Water Margin)*	C	N	R/M	9-12
Silva, José *Asunción nocturno*	S	PI	E	9-12
Steinbeck, John *Las uvas de la ira (The Grapes of Wrath)*	S	N	C	9-12
Storni, Alfonsina *Hombre pequeñito (The Little Man)*	S	PI	E	9-12

Material	Language	Type of literature	Type of entry	Grade span
Takamura, Kootaroo *Boroboro na dachoo*	J	PI	C	11-12
Thoreau, Henry David *Walden, or Life in the Woods*	C	NF	C	9-11
Trang, Chau *Y si tien tuyen (The Frontline Physician)*	V	E	E	9-12
Trang, Ngea *Ariyathar Khmer (The Khmer Civilization)*	Kh	E	C	11-12
Twain, Mark *The Autobiography of Mark Twain*	C	B	C	9-11
Vang, Lue, and Judy Lewis *Grandmother's Path, Grandfather's Way*	Hm	F	R/M	9-10
Vargas-Llosa, Mario *La literatura es fuego (Literature Is Fire)*	S	E	E	11-12
Vasconcelos, José *La raza cósmica (The Cosmic Race)*	S	E	C	9-12
Vega, Lope F. de *Fuenteovejuna (The Sheep Well)*	S	D	E	10-12
Vu, Khac Khoan *Than thap rua (The Turtle Tower God)*	V	FM	C	9-12
Vu Ngoc Phan *Nha van hien dai (The Contemporary Writers)*	V	B	C	9-12
Wang Yu (Ed.) *Selected Poems by Overseas Chinese Writers*	C	PA	R/M	11-12
Wu Cheng'en *Journey to the West (or Monkey)*	C	N	R/M	11-12
Xin, Bin *Selected Works of Bin Xin*	C	E	E	9-12
Yum, Sang-Sub *Selected Works of Yum, Sang-Sub*	K	SS	E	9-12
Zhang Cuo (Dominic Cheung) *Golden Tears*	C	NF	E	9-12

RECREATIONAL AND MOTIVATIONAL MATERIALS

THIS section presents a list of recreational and motivational materials. Teachers and members of selection committees for school districts' materials can use the list to select books for students' independent reading, both in the classroom and for leisure-time reading.

The list includes titles that accommodate a broad range of reading interests, and it incorporates works of special appeal to individual readers as well as works that have universal appeal. Hopefully, students will discover new authors from the list.

When the entry concerns literary contributions of specific ethnic or cultural groups, the ethnic or cultural group is indicated. The groups are identified by the following symbols:

B—Black
C—Chinese
F—Filipino
H—Hispanic
Hm—Hmong
I—American Indian

J—Japanese
K—Korean
Kh—Khmer
S—Samoan
V—Vietnamese

No grade level has been indicated for the list so that teachers, librarians, and members of selection committees can determine the most effective use of the works for specific readers. Further, teachers, librarians, and members of selection committees are enthusiastically encouraged to update the list with new titles as they are published and additional works that are appropriate to individual school situations.

Material	Culture
Biographies	
Alford, Terry *Prince Among Slaves*	B
Allen, Maury *Jackie Robinson: A Life Remembered*	B
Andrews, Lynn V. *Medicine Woman*	I
Ashe, Arthur, and Neil Amdur *Off the Court*	
Bleier, Rocky, and Terry O'Neil *Fighting Back*	
Bourke-White, Margaret *Portrait of Myself*	
Buchanan, William J. *A Shining Season: The True Story of John Baker*	
Campanella, Roy *It's Good to Be Alive*	B
Carrighar, Sally *Home to the Wilderness*	
Chaplik, Dorothy *Up with Hope: A Biography of Jesse Jackson*	B
Collier, James Lincoln *Louis Armstrong: An American Success Story*	B
Criddle, Joan D., and Teeda Butt Mam *To Destroy You Is No Loss: The Odyssey of a Cambodian Family*	Kh
Dahl, Roald *Going Solo*	
Fido, Martin *Shakespeare*	

Material	Culture
Frances, Clare *Woman Alone: Sailing Solo Across the Atlantic*	
Gilbreth, Frank B., and Ernestine Carey *Cheaper by the Dozen*	
Graham, Robin L., and L.T. Gill *Dove*	
Grant, Glen, and Dennis Ogawa *Ellison Onizuka: A Remembrance*	J
Hughes, Langston *The Big Sea*	B
Jenkins, Peter, and Barbara Jenkins *The Walk West: A Walk Across America*	
Kerr, M.E. *Me, Me, Me, Me, Me: Not a Novel*	
Killilea, Marie *Karen*	
Lynn, Loretta, and George Vecsey *Coal Miner's Daughter*	
Martinez, Max *The Adventures of the Chicano Kid and Other Stories*	H
Meltzer, Milton *Adolf Hitler: A Portrait in Tyranny*	
Mendheim, Beverly A. *Ritchie Valens: The First Latino Rocker*	H
Milford, Nancy *Zelda: A Biography*	
Morris, Jeannie *Brian Piccolo: A Short Season*	
Peck, Richard E. *Something for Joey*	
Perera, Victor *Rites: A Guatemalan Boyhood*	H

Material	Culture
Poitier, Sidney *This Life*	B
Reiss, Johanna *The Upstairs Room*	
Retton, Mary Lou, and Bela Karolyi *Mary Lou: Creating an Olympic Gymnast*	
Siegal, Aranka *Upon the Head of the Goat: A Childhood in Hungary*	
Specht, Robert *Tisha: Story of a Young Teacher in the Alaska Wilderness*	
Stevenson, Fanny, and Robert Louis Stevenson *Our Samoan Adventure*	S
Stone, Irving *Sailor on Horseback*	
Valens, Evans G. *A Long Way up: The Story of Jill Kinmont*	
Valens, Evans G. *The Other Side of the Mountain*	
Vinke, Hermann *The Short Life of Sophie Scholl*	
Wiener, Jon *Come Together: John Lennon in His Time*	
Wolfe, Tom *The Right Stuff*	
Yeager, Chuck, and Leo Janos *Yeager: An Autobiography*	
Zaharias, Babe Didrikson *This Life I've Led*	

Material	Culture
Drama	
Bart, Lionel *Oliver!*	
Blinn, William *Brian's Song*	
Brown, William, and Charlie Small *Wiz*	B
Casey, Warren, and Jim Jacobs *Grease*	
Chase, Mary *Harvey*	
Christie, Agatha *The Mousetrap and Other Plays*	
Darion, Joe, and Dale Wasserman *Man of La Mancha*	
Ebb, Fred, and others *Cabaret*	
Eliot, T.S. *Cats: The Book of the Musical*	
Hauptman, William, and Roger Miller *Big River: The Adventures of Huckleberry Finn*	

Material	Culture
Drama—(Continued)	
Henley, Beth *Crimes of the Heart*	
Laurents, Arthur *West Side Story*	
Lerner, Alan J., and Frederick Loewe *Camelot*	
Lindsay, Howard, with Richard Rodgers and Oscar Hammerstein II *Oklahoma*	
Rose, Reginald *Dino*	
Sackler, Howard *Great White Hope*	B
Shaffer, Anthony *Sleuth*	
Stein, Joseph, and others *Fiddler on the Roof*	
Willson, Meredith, and Richard Morris *Music Man*	

Material	Culture
Folklore and Mythology	
Bradley, Marion Zimmer *The Mists of Avalon*	
Brindel, June *Phaedra: A Novel of Ancient Athens*	
Coburn, Jewell R. *Khmers, Tigers, and Talismans: From the History and Legends of Mysterious Cambodia*	Kh
Coburn, Jewell R., and Quyen Van Duong *Beyond the East Wind: Legends and Folktales of Vietnam*	V
Johnson, Charles *Hmong Folktales Retold in English*	Hm
Philip, Neil (as told by) *The Tale of Sir Gawain*	
Pyle, Howard *The Story of King Arthur and His Knights*	
Renault, Mary *The King Must Die*	
Ruoff, Mona *From the Dragon's Cloud: Vietnamese Folktales*	V
Stewart, Mary *The Crystal Cave*	
Stone, Merlin *Ancient Mirrors of Womanhood: A Treasury of Goddess and Heroine Lore from Around the World*	
Sutcliff, Rosemary *The Road to Camlann: The Death of King Arthur*	
Van Der Veer, Judy *To the Rescue*	I

Material	Culture
Nonfiction	
Belting, Natalia *Our Fathers Had Powerful Songs*	I
Bishop, Jim *The Day Lincoln Was Shot*	
Braymer, Marjorie *Atlantis: The Biography of a Legend*	
Brickhill, Paul *The Great Escape*	
Campbell, Margaret *From the Hands of the Hills*	Hm
Caputo, Philip *A Rumor of War*	V
Cousteau, Jacques, and Frederic Dumas *The Silent World*	
Coutant, Helen *First Snow*	V
Dunn, Mary L. *Man in the Box: A Story from Vietnam*	V
Edelman, Bernard (Ed.) *Dear America: Letters Home from Vietnam*	
Ellerbee, Linda *And So It Goes: Adventures in Television*	

Material	Culture
Fossey, Diane *Gorillas in the Mist*	
Garcia Marquez, Gabriel *Clandestine in Chile: The Adventures of Miguel Littin*	H
Henry, Will *From Where the Sun Now Stands*	
Heyerdahl, Thor *Kon-Tiki*	
Houston, James D. *Californians*	
Johanson, Donald C., and Maitland A. Edey *Lucy: The Beginnings of Humankind*	
Josephy, Alvin M., Jr. *Now That the Buffalo's Gone*	I
Kazimiroff, Theodore L. *The Last Algonquin*	I
Levin, Meyer *Compulsion*	
Lewis, Anthony *Gideon's Trumpet*	
Lord, Walter *Night to Remember*	
Mowat, Farley *Never Cry Wolf*	
Ngan, Nguyen N. *Will of Heaven: A Story of One Vietnamese and the End of His World*	V
Ngor, Haing, and Roger Warner *Haing Ngor: A Cambodian Odyssey*	Kh

Material	Culture
Nonfiction—(Continued)	
North, James *Freedom Rising*	B
Pace, Mildred *Wrapped for Eternity: The Story of the Egyptian Mummy*	
Radin, Edward D. *Lizzie Borden: The Untold Story*	
Rather, Dan, and Mickey Herskowitz *The Camera Never Blinks: Adventures of a TV Journalist*	
Rylant, Cynthia *Every Living Thing*	
Valladares, Armando *Against All Hope: The Prison Memoirs of Armando Valladares*	H
Wyden, Peter *Day One: Before Hiroshima and After*	J
Yathay, Pin, and John Man *Stay Alive, My Son*	Kh

Material	Culture
Novels	
Adams, Douglas *The Hitchhiker's Guide to the Galaxy*	
Adams, Richard *Watership Down*	
Alexander, Lloyd *Westmark*	
Allende, Isabel *The House of the Spirits*	H
Anaya, Rudolfo A. *Heart of Aztlan*	H
Anderson, Joan *Seventeen Eighty-Seven*	
Angell, Judie *One Way to Ansonia*	
Anthony, Piers *A Spell for Chameleon*	
Arenas, Reinaldo *Farewell to the Sea*	H
Arrick, Fran *Tunnel Vision*	
Asher, Sandy *Missing Pieces*	
Asimov, Isaac *Foundation*	
Auel, Jean M. *The Clan of the Cave Bear*	
Avi *Wolf Rider*	
Baldwin, James *If Beale Street Could Talk*	B
Ball, John *In the Heat of the Night*	

Material	Culture
Barrett, William *The Lilies of the Field*	B
Barrio, Raymond *The Plum Plum Pickers*	H
Beagle, Peter S. *Last Unicorn*	
Bell, Clare *Ratha's Creature*	
Bennett, Jack *The Voyage of the Lucky Dragon*	V
Bennett, Jay *Say Hello to the Hit Man*	
Bess, Clayton *Tracks*	
Bethancourt, T. Ernesto *Where the Deer and the Canteloupe Play*	H
Blessing, Richard *A Passing Season*	
Blos, Joan *Brothers of the Heart*	
Bonham, Frank *Durango Street*	
Bradbury, Ray *Dandelion Wine*	
Bradford, Richard *Red Sky at Morning*	
Brancato, Robin *Sweet Bells Jangled Out of Tune*	
Bredes, Don *Hard Feelings*	
Brent, Madeleine *Merlin's Keep*	

Material	Culture
Bridgers, Sue Ellen *Home Before Dark*	
Brooks, Bruce *The Moves Make the Man*	B
Brown, Dee *Creek Mary's Blood*	I
Brown, Roy *Cage*	
Bunting, Eve *If I Asked You, Would You Stay?*	
Burns, Olive A. *Cold Sassy Tree*	
Card, Orson S. *Ender's Game*	
Chandler, Raymond *Farewell, My Lovely*	
Childress, Alice *A Hero Ain't Nothin' but a Sandwich*	B
Christie, Agatha *And Then There Were None*	
Christopher, John *The White Mountains*	
Clapp, Patricia *Witches' Children*	

Material	Culture
Novels—(Continued)	
Clarke, Arthur C. *Two Thousand and One: A Space Odyssey*	
Cleaver, Vera, and Bill Cleaver *Where the Lilies Bloom*	
Conrad, Pamela *Prairie Songs*	
Conroy, Pat *The Prince of Tides*	
Cooper, Susan *The Grey King*	
Corcoran, Barbara *Clown*	
Cross, Gillian *Born of the Sun*	
Crutcher, Chris *Stotan!*	
Cummings, Betty S. *Now, Ameriky*	
Cunningham, Julia *Burnish Me Bright*	
Danziger, Paula *Can You Sue Your Parents for Malpractice?*	
Davis, Jenny *Good-bye and Keep Cold*	
Degens, T. *Transport 741-R*	
Dickinson, Peter *Gift*	
Dickson, Gordon R. *The Dragon and the George*	

Material	Culture
Dixon, Paige *May I Cross Your Golden River?*	
Doctorow, E.L. *Ragtime*	
Donaldson, Stephen R. *Lord Foul's Bane: The Chronicles of Thomas Covenant, the Unbeliever*	
Dorris, Michael *A Yellow Raft in Blue Water*	I
Doyle, Arthur Conan *The Hound of the Baskervilles*	
Du Maurier, Daphne *Rebecca*	
Duncan, Lois *Summer of Fear*	
Durham, Marilyn *Man Who Loved Cat Dancing*	
Engdahl, Sylvia L. *Enchantress from the Stars*	
Ferris, Jean *Invincible Summer*	
Finney, Jack *Time and Again*	
Fleischman, Paul *Rear-View Mirrors*	
Forman, James *People of the Dream*	I
Forsyth, Frederick *The Day of the Jackal*	
Fowles, John *The Collector*	
Fox, Paula *The Moonlight Man*	

Material	Culture
Freedman, Benedict, and Nancy Freedman *Mrs. Mike*	
French, Michael *Pursuit*	
Fuentes, Carlos *The Old Gringo*	H
Gaines, Ernest J. *A Gathering of Old Men*	B
Garcia, Lionel *A Shroud in the Family*	H
Gardam, Jane *Hollow Land*	
Garden, Nancy *Annie on My Mind*	
Gehrts, Barbara *Don't Say a Word*	
Girion, Barbara *A Handful of Stars*	
Godden, Rumer *China Court*	
Goldman, William *The Princess Bride*	
Guy, Rosa *Edith Jackson*	
Haley, Alex *Roots*	B
Hall, Lynn *The Solitary*	
Hamilton, Virginia *Sweet Whispers, Brother Rush*	B
Hansen, Joyce *Home Boy*	H/B

Material	Culture
Harris, Marilyn *Hatter Fox*	I
Hautzig, Deborah *Second Star to the Right*	
Hayden, Torey L. *The Sunflower Forest*	
Hentoff, Nat *Jazz Country*	
Herbert, Frank *Dune*	
Heyer, Georgette *The Grand Sophy*	
Hill, Douglas *Young Legionary*	
Hillerman, Tony *The Blessing Way*	I
Hogan, William *Quartzsite Trip*	
Holland, Isabelle *The Man Without a Face*	
Holman, Felice *Slake's Limbo*	
Holt, Victoria *Menfreya in the Morning*	
Horowitz, Anthony *The Devil's Doorbell*	
Howker, Janni *The Nature of the Beast*	
Hunt, Irene *No Promises in the Wind*	
Hunter, Mollie *A Sound of Chariots*	

Material	Culture
Novels—(Continued)	
Irwin, Hadley *Abby, My Love*	
James, P.D. *Death of an Expert Witness*	
Johnson, Dorothy M. *A Man Called Horse*	I
Jones, Diana W. *Howl's Moving Castle*	
Jones, Douglas C. *Season of Yellow Leaf*	I
Jones, Toeckey *Skindeep*	B
Jordan, June *His Own Where*	B
Kazantzakis, Nikos *Zorba the Greek*	
Kelley, William M. *Different Drummer*	B
Kogawa, Joy *Obasan*	J
Konigsburg, E.L. *A Proud Taste for Scarlet and Miniver*	
Laguerre, Enrique *The Labyrinth*	H
L'Amour, Louis *Day Breakers*	
Lasky, Kathryn *Pageant*	
Lawrence, Louise *Children of the Dust*	
LeGuin, Ursula K. *The Wizard of Earthsea*	

Material	Culture
L'Engle, Madeleine *A House Like a Lotus*	
Lesley, Craig *Winterkill*	I
Magorian, Michelle *Good Night, Mr. Tom*	
Mahy, Margaret *Memory*	
Malamud, Bernard *Natural*	
Mark, Jan *Handles*	
Mason, Bobbie A. *In Country*	
Mathis, Sharon B. *Listen for the Fig Tree*	B
Mayne, William *Earthfasts*	
Mays, Lucinda *Other Shore*	
Mazer, Norma F. *After the Rain*	
Mazer, Norma F., and Harry Mazer *The Solid Gold Kid*	
McCaffrey, Anne *Dragonflight*	
McKinley, Robin *The Hero and the Crown*	
Michener, James A. *Sayonara*	
Miklowitz, Gloria D. *Close to the Edge*	

Material	Culture
Miller, Frances A. *Truth Trap*	
Mitchell, Margaret *Gone with the Wind*	
Mohr, Nicholasa *In Nueva York*	H/B
Momaday, N. Scott *Owl in the Cedar Tree*	I
Morrison, Toni *Sula*	B
Murphy, Jim *Death Run*	
Murphy, Shirley R. *Nightpool*	
Murrow, Liza K. *West Against the Wind*	
Myers, Walter D. *Fallen Angels*	
Neufeld, John *Lisa, Bright and Dark*	
Newton, Suzanne *I Will Call It Georgie's Blues*	
Nixon, Joan L. *The Stalker*	
O'Brien, Robert C. *Z for Zachariah*	
O'Neal, Zibby *In Summer Light*	
Paterson, Katherine *Jacob Have I Loved*	
Patterson, Sarah *The Distant Summer*	

Material	Culture
Paulsen, Gary *Hatchet*	I
Peck, Richard *Princess Ashley*	
Peters, Ellis *A Morbid Taste for Bones*	
Petry, Ann *Tituba of Salem Village*	B
Peyton, K.M. *A Midsummer Night's Death*	
Pfeffer, Susan B. *The Year Without Michael*	
Phipson, Joan *Hit and Run*	
Pierce, Meredith *The Darkangel*	
Pullman, Philip *The Ruby in the Smoke*	
Raucher, Herman *Summer of Forty-Two*	
Rice, Anne *Interview with the Vampire*	
Rinaldi, Ann *Time Enough for Drums*	
Rockwood, Joyce *To Spoil the Sun*	I

Material	Culture
Novels—(Continued)	
Rostkowski, Margaret I. *After the Dancing Days*	
Ruby, Lois *This Old Man*	
St. Claire Robson, Lucia *Walk in My Soul*	I
Sandoz, Mari *The Horsecatcher*	I
Scoppettone, Sandra *The Late Great Me*	
Sebestyen, Ouida *Words by Heart*	B
Sender, Ruth M. *The Cage*	
Shange, Ntozake *Betsey Brown*	B
Shute, Nevil *A Town Like Alice*	
Sleator, William *Interstellar Pig*	
Smith, Betty *A Tree Grows in Brooklyn*	
Snyder, Zilpha K. *The Birds of Summer*	
Spark, Muriel *The Prime of Miss Jean Brodie*	
Stewart, Mary *The Moon-Spinners*	
Stone, Bruce *Half Nelson, Full Nelson*	

Material	Culture
Strasser, Todd *Friends till the End*	
Swarthout, Glendon *Bless the Beasts and Children*	
Taylor, Mildred D. *Let the Circle Be Unbroken*	B
Tevis, Walter *The Queen's Gambit*	
Tey, Josephine *The Daughter of Time*	
Thomas, Joyce C. *Marked by Fire*	B
Townsend, John R. *The Creatures*	
Townsend, Sue *The Secret Diary of Adrian Mole*	
Uhlman, Fred *Reunion*	
Uris, Leon *Exodus*	
Van Der Post, Laurens *A Story Like the Wind*	
Verne, Jules *Twenty Thousand Leagues Under the Sea*	
Villasenor, Edmund *Macho!*	H
Voigt, Cynthia *Izzy, Willy-Nilly*	
Walker, Margaret *Jubilee*	B
Wallin, Luke *In the Shadow of the Wind*	I

Material	Culture
Walsh, Jill P. *Fireweed*	
Walter, Mildred P. *Because We Are*	B
Wartski, Maureen C. *A Boat to Nowhere*	V
Welch, James *Fools Crow*	I
Wersba, Barbara *Tunes for a Small Harmonica*	
Westall, Robert *The Scarecrows*	
White, Robb *Deathwatch*	
Wilkinson, Brenda *Ludell and Willie*	B
Williams, Sherley A. *Dessa Rose*	B
Wisler, G. Clifton *Thunder on the Tennessee*	
Wojciechowska, Maia *Tuned Out*	
Wolitzer, Meg *Caribou*	
Wrightson, Patricia *A Little Fear*	
Yep, Laurence *Sea Glass*	C
Yolen, Jane *Dragon's Blood*	
Zelazny, Roger *Nine Princes in Amber*	

Poetry Collections

Material	Culture
Bruchac, Joseph (Ed.) *Songs from This Earth on Turtle's Back: An Anthology of Poetry by American Indian Writers*	I
Dodge, Robert K., and Joseph B. McCullough *New and Old Voices of Wah' Kon-Tah*	I
Flores, Joseph A. (Ed.) *Songs and Dreams*	H
Giovanni, Nikki *Black Feeling, Black Talk, Black Judgment*	B
Glenn, Mel *Class Dismissed! High School Poems*	
Gonzales, Rodolfo *I Am Joaquin*	H
Gordon, Ruth (Ed.) *Under All Silences: The Many Shades of Love*	H
Highwater, Jamake (Ed.) *Words in the Blood: Contemporary Indian Writers of North and South America*	I

Material	Culture
Poetry Collections—(Continued)	
Hopkins, Lee B. (Ed.) *Love and Kisses*	
Jones, Hettie (Ed.) *Trees Stand Shining*	I
Knudson, R.R, and May Swenson (Eds.) *American Sports Poems*	
Larrick, Nancy (Ed.) *Bring Me All of Your Dreams*	
Lee, Laurie *As I Walked Out One Midsummer Morning*	
Lorde, Audre *The Black Unicorn*	B
Merriam, Eve *If Only I Could Tell You: Poems for Young Lovers and Dreamers*	
Nash, Ogden *Custard and Company*	

Material	Culture
Short-Story Collections	
791.43/9 Asimov, Isaac *I, Robot*	
Baldwin, James *Going to Meet the Man*	B
Bradbury, Ray *Golden Apples of the Sun*	
Gaines, Ernest J. *Bloodline*	B
Gallo, Donald R. (Ed.) *Sixteen: Short Stories by Outstanding Writers for Young Adults*	
King, Stephen *Skeleton Crew*	
Konigsburg, E.L. *Throwing Shadows*	
Lester, Julius *This Strange New Feeling*	B
Mark, Jan *Nothing to Be Afraid Of*	
McCord, Jean *Bitter Is the Hawk's Path*	
Mohr, Nicholasa *El Bronx Remembered: A Novella and Stories*	H
Sargent, Pamela (Ed.) *Women of Wonder: Science Fiction Stories by Women About Women*	
Thomas, Piri *Stories from El Barrio*	H
Trambley, Estela P. *Rain of Scorpions*	H
Washington, Mary H. (Ed.) *Black-Eyed Susans: Classic Stories by and About Black Women*	B

Appendix

Storytelling: An Evocative Approach to Literature

By Catharine Farrell*

Zellerbach Family Fund Consultant,
Language Arts and Foreign Languages Unit,
California State Department of Education

S TORYTELLING for high school students? Some people might think that an unlikely idea. One person's experiences with storytelling might conjure up a memory of grandmother in her rocking chair or the librarian giving a quiet story hour in the children's room. Another person might recall a spine-chilling story told around the campfire with the scouts. Storytelling seems, at first glance, a pastime for a more innocent age and era.

But such is distinctly not the case. Today's teenagers are extremely demanding and sophisticated and so is storytelling. The work of the story-teller is intense, intricate, and personal. Telling portions of literary works to a high school English class—rather than reading aloud from the text—requires considerable inner concentration and interpretive skill. The teller must prepare for the storytelling of a text directly to the students. In an audience of high school students, some students may be initially shy in a storytelling situation, but they will have tremendous respect for the teller.

In the immediacy of a storytelling session, time seems to stop. The teller creates an environment free from distractions, maintains continuous eye contact, and speaks directly to the listeners. The images from the story appear to hang in the air, and the silence in the classroom deepens. All the students become engrossed in the shared experience of literature.

The heightened attention to a literary work created by storytelling has many teaching possibilities. Each teacher should try to develop a repertoire of literary pieces for storytelling. As teachers discover the compelling nature of storytelling as a teaching method, they will be greatly rewarded for their efforts.

Many high school teachers of literature are using storytelling with great success throughout California. Of note are the efforts of the administrators and teachers of ABC Unified School District, Cerritos, Los Angeles County. Recent experience of these educators and others has provided a clear direction in the use and benefit of storytelling in high school literature classes.

Storytelling provides equal access to great literary works.

FOR those students who are not able to read a text easily, storytelling brings this text to life in a particularly dramatic way. These students include the limited-English-speaking students, the newcomers from other lands, the remedial students, and the underachieving students. The profound interpretation of the text by the teacher/storyteller—using hand gestures, facial expressions, and precise dialogue—gives these students the extra clues to comprehension that they often need. In addition, these students experience the universal truths of the literary work firsthand and are greatly motivated to read through the text for themselves.

Field example: Before students were introduced to a literary selection, the teacher told the following stories: Act I, Scene I, from *Hamlet*; the "Wife of Bath's Tale" and the "Pardoner's Tale" from *The Canterbury Tales*; and "A Tree. A Rock. A Cloud." from an anthology of short stories by Carson McCullers. Discussion, illustration, and creative writing followed the storytelling session. The students maintained a high interest level in the other tales, stories, and scenes from the literary selection.

Storytelling can provide the framework for the literary work.

THE storytelling of the entire work or significant portions of the work gives students an expert knowledge of the plot line and sequence of action. If the teacher/storyteller remains true to the sequence of action and carefully reproduces the unfolding plot, the students can struggle through often difficult language with greater contextual comprehension.

Field example: Teachers told the story of the entire drama of *Julius Caesar;* the culminating courtroom scene from *The Merchant of Venice;* the entire short story of "The Lottery" by Shirley Jackson; and selected segments from Joseph Conrad's *Heart of Darkness.* Discussions following these storytelling sessions and subsequent reading assignments evidenced a higher level of comprehension of the real life issues facing the characters, the moral and ethical questions being raised, and the clear outcome of action. The students' comprehension was significantly greater than that in discussions following a reading assignment given for the same material.

Storytelling allows students to respond directly to content.

B ECAUSE the entire class shares the immediate listening experience of hearing the literary work being told to them, all students feel qualified to enter into a dynamic discussion of the important issues of the text.

Field example: The storytelling of O. Henry's "The Last Leaf" brought forth a provocative discussion of death, hope, and transference, as well as personal experience stories, from students who previously had been left out. A creative writing assignment flowed easily and naturally from this language-rich activity that included listening and speaking.

Storytelling promotes a closer reading of the text.

B ECAUSE the students have a natural grasp of the plot sequence and the outcome of the action, they are able to focus on details of the text that are usually abandoned. The teacher/storyteller uses details of action to condense action. Using storytelling technique as a model, the students are creatively interested in the twists and turns of the text.

Field examples: (1) The storytelling of one short story by Carson McCullers ("A Tree. A Rock. A Cloud.") showed that students were enthusiastic in supporting their discussion points by a close reading of the text. This same enthusiasm was not present in their next class session in which there was no storytelling. (2) Storytelling segments from each chapter of Kurt Vonnegut's *Slaughterhouse-Five* allowed students to focus on the novel's events, which they learned about in the previous day's reading assignment. The students had a lively discussion of the novel, and they demonstrated vivid recall of each chapter.

Storytelling creates visual images of the piece in the students' minds.

S TUDENTS are able to see the people, places, and events in the story as if they were eyewitnesses to the experience. This is more likely to occur with storytelling than with reading aloud because the teacher/storyteller is concentrating on the visual images in order to tell the story.

Field examples: (1) After hearing the Afro-American slave story, *The People Could Fly,* by Virginia Hamilton, high school art students drew vivid and interpretive renderings of the events in the story. Each student's drawing was unique and infused with a deep emotional comprehension of the work. (2) After a storytelling of "A View of Death," a chapter from William Golding's *Lord of the Flies,* students were easily able to discuss the symbolic nature of the beginning stages of a storm as described in the chapter. (3) After hearing the firsthand account of the bombing of Hiroshima (August 6, 1945) retold by their teacher from Toshi Maruki's autobiography, *Hiroshima no pika,* students had an unforgettable impression of the events of that day and the days that followed. They were able to draw evocative scenes from the storytelling and to discuss the issues of nuclear war. This storytelling session was used to introduce the students to a unit on "The Victims of War" and to the book *Hiroshima,* by John Hersey.

Storytelling enhances the students' ability to hear literature as they read it themselves.

H IGH school students often cannot hear the voice of the author as they read. Subtle points, such as satire and irony, are lost in the understanding of the piece. This lack inhibits the students' own writing style because they do not hear themselves speaking as they write.

Field example: The storytelling of Mark Twain's "Celebrated Jumping Frog of Calaveras County" gave students an unmistakable appreciation of Twain's wit in his writing the entire hilarious tale in the deadpan, earnest voice of Simon Wheeler. Students were then asked to tell the funniest experience of their life in a similar deadpan voice to a partner. Their understanding of Twain's use of voice in his works assisted their readings of *The Adventures of Huckleberry Finn* and, later, a more recent American novel, *The Catcher in the Rye,* by J.D. Salinger.

Storytelling explores multicultural literature from the oral tradition.

T EACHERS and students open new doors when they restore the oral tradition to the high school literature program. Teachers can present the classic myths and legends in their original form, and students can bring to class the traditional tales told to them by their family members. Teachers have the unprecedented opportunity to retrieve the folktales of newcomers from such places as Southeast Asia and Central and South America. Along with collecting these tales from newcomers, teachers can add to the curriculum the students' family stories as well as local legends and modern lore. Finally, students can write their own versions of traditional tales.

Field examples: (1) After hearing a cycle of *pourquoi* tales (how things came to be the way they are), one high school class wrote a series of original *pourquoi* tales. All students participated in writing these stories, an unusual occurrence for this class. (2) After students heard a teacher's telling of his original spine-chilling short story, they were then able to compose their own original tales, working in small groups and taking turns reading their stories aloud.

Storytelling encourages students to become storytellers.

F INALLY, by hearing stories told to them, students are motivated to tell stories themselves. They appreciate and respect the storyteller's art. Becoming storytellers will aid them with their social skills and parenting skills, increase their ability to think on their feet, and develop their natural communication skills in all phases of their lives.

Field example: High school students who have formed a Storytelling Club have sponsored a float in the Homecoming Parade, have told their favorite stories in the elementary and middle schools in their district, and have visited the senior citizen center to tell as well as hear stories.

Stories are the thread of life, and their appeal is ageless and timeless.

T O reach today's adolescents with the universal messages of great literature is a wonderful task. Storytelling is as powerful a teaching tool in today's world as ever and it is, perhaps, now even more important.

The author of *Storytelling: An Evocative Approach to Literature* would like to thank the following teachers, librarians, and administrators who field-tested storytelling as a teaching method in the curriculum for grades nine through twelve:

In Contra Costa County at Las Lomas High School, Walnut Creek—John Blake, Librarian; Rhio Ossola, Drama Teacher; and Corinda Barbour, Betty Gerber, Diane Inman, Marie Kahn, Marshall Pfeiffer, and Janene Scovel of the English Department; and at Alhambra High School, Martinez, Patricia Hamilton-Bolds, Librarian.

In Los Angeles County, ABC Unified School District—Dorothy Crandall and Helen Fried, administrators; at Cerritos High School, Meg Booth, Maggie Brauner, Ray Brown, Pat Ray, Janet Steger, and Don Teague, of the English Department; at Whitney High School, Cerritos, Marli Surjopolis, English Teacher; and at Tetzlaff Junior High School, Cerritos, Dorothy M. Farrow, English teacher and coauthor of the ABC Unified School District's *Storytelling Handbook for Grades Seven Through Twelve.*

Index of Authors

Index of Titles

C

T

W

Y

Z

Publications Available from the Department of Education

This publication is one of over 650 that are available from the California State Department of Education. Some of the more recent publications or those most widely used are the following:

ISBN	Title (Date of publication)	Price
0-8011-0271-5	Academic Honesty (1986)	$2.50
0-8011-0722-9	Accounting Procedures for Student Organizations (1988)	3.75
0-8011-0272-3	Administration of Maintenance and Operations in California School Districts (1986)	6.75
0-8011-0216-2	Bilingual-Crosscultural Teacher Aides: A Resource Guide (1984)	3.50
0-8011-0238-3	Boating the Right Way (1985)	4.00
0-8011-0275-8	California Dropouts: A Status Report (1986)	2.50
0-8011-0783-0	California Private School Directory, 1988-89 (1988)	14.00
0-8011-0747-4	California Public School Directory (1989)	14.00
0-8011-0748-2	California School Accounting Manual (1988)	8.00
0-8011-0715-6	California Women: Activities Guide, K—12 (1988)	3.50
0-8011-0488-2	Caught in the Middle: Educational Reform for Young Adolescents in California Public Schools (1987)	5.00
0-8011-0760-1	Celebrating the National Reading Initiative (1989)	6.75
0-8011-0777-6	The Changing Mathematics Curriculum: A Booklet for Parents (1989)	10 for 5.00
0-8011-0241-3	Computer Applications Planning (1985)	5.00
0-8011-0823-3	Coordinated Compliance Monitoring Review Manual, 1989-90 (1989)	6.75
0-8011-0797-0	Desktop Publishing Guidelines (1989)	4.00
0-8011-0749-0	Educational Software Preview Guide, 1988-89 (1988)	2.00
0-8011-0489-0	Effective Practices in Achieving Compensatory Education-Funded Schools II (1987)	5.00
0-8011-0041-0	English–Language Arts Framework for California Public Schools (1987)	3.00
0-8011-0731-8	English–Language Arts Model Curriculum Guide, K—8 (1988)	3.00
0-8011-0786-5	Enrichment Opportunities Guide: A Resource for Teachers and Students in Mathematics and Science (1988)	8.75
0-8011-0710-5	Family Life/Sex Education Guidelines (1987)	4.00
0-8011-0804-7	Foreign Language Framework for California Public Schools (1989)	5.50
0-8011-0751-2	First Moves: Welcoming a Child to a New Caregiving Setting (videocassette and guide) (1988)*	65.00
0-8011-0289-8	Handbook for Physical Education (1986)	4.50
0-8011-0249-9	Handbook for Planning an Effective Foreign Language Program (1985)	3.50
0-8011-0320-7	Handbook for Planning an Effective Literature Program (1987)	3.00
0-8011-0179-4	Handbook for Planning an Effective Mathematics Program (1982)	2.00
0-8011-0290-1	Handbook for Planning an Effective Writing Program (1986)	2.50
0-8011-0824-1	Handbook for Teaching Cantonese-Speaking Students (1989)	4.50
0-8011-0680-x	Handbook for Teaching Japanese-Speaking Students (1987)	4.50
0-8011-0291-x	Handbook for Teaching Pilipino-Speaking Students (1986)	4.50
0-8011-0825-x	Handbook for Teaching Portuguese-Speaking Students (1989)	4.50
0-8011-0250-2	Handbook on California Education for Language Minority Parents—Chinese/English Edition (1985)†	3.25
0-8011-0737-7	Here They Come: Ready or Not—Report of the School Readiness Task Force (Summary) (1988)	2.00
0-8011-0734-2	Here They Come: Ready or Not—Report of the School Readiness Task Force (Full Report) (1988)	4.25
0-8011-0735-0	Here They Come: Ready or Not—Appendixes to the Full Report of the School Readiness Task Force (1988)	22.50
0-8011-0712-1	History–Social Science Framework for California Public Schools (1988)	6.00
0-8011-0782-2	Images: A Workbook for Enhancing Self-esteem and Promoting Career Preparation, Especially for Black Girls (1989)	6.00
0-8011-0750-4	Infant/Toddler Caregiving: An Annotated Guide to Media Training Materials (1989)	8.75
0-8011-0466-1	Instructional Patterns: Curriculum for Parenthood Education (1985)	12.00
0-8011-0828-4	Instructor's Behind-the-Wheel Guide for California's Bus Driver's Training Course (1989)	20.00
0-8011-0208-1	Manual of First-Aid Practices for School Bus Drivers (1983)	1.75
0-8011-0209-x	Martin Luther King, Jr., 1929—1968 (1983)	3.25
0-8011-0358-4	Mathematics Framework for California Public Schools (1985)	3.00
0-8011-0664-8	Mathematics Model Curriculum Guide, K—8 (1987)	2.75
0-8011-0725-3	Model Curriculum for Human Rights and Genocide (1988)	3.25
0-8011-0252-9	Model Curriculum Standards: Grades 9—12 (1985)	5.50
0-8011-0762-8	Moral and Civic Education and Teaching About Religion (1988)	3.25
0-8011-0229-4	Nutrition Education—Choose Well, Be Well: A Curriculum Guide for Junior High School (1984)	8.00
0-8011-0228-6	Nutrition Education—Choose Well, Be Well: A Curriculum Guide for High School (1984)	8.00
0-8011-0182-4	Nutrition Education—Choose Well, Be Well: A Curriculum Guide for Preschool and Kindergarten (1982)	8.00
0-8011-0183-2	Nutrition Education—Choose Well, Be Well: A Curriculum Guide for the Primary Grades (1982)	8.00
0-8011-0184-0	Nutrition Education—Choose Well, Be Well: A Curriculum Guide for the Upper Elementary Grades (1982)	8.00
0-8011-0230-8	Nutrition Education—Choose Well, Be Well: A Resource Manual for Parent and Community Involvement in Nutrition Education Programs (1984)	4.50

*Videocassette also available in Chinese (Cantonese) and Spanish at the same price.
†The following editions are also available, at the same price: Armenian/English, Cambodian/English, Hmong/English, Japanese/English, Korean/English, Laotian/English, Pilipino/English, Spanish/English, and Vietnamese/English.

ISBN	Title (Date of publication)	Price
0-8011-0185-9	Nutrition Education—Choose Well, Be Well: A Resource Manual for Preschool, Kindergarten, and Elementary Teachers (1982)	$2.25
0-8011-0186-7	Nutrition Education—Choose Well, Be Well: A Resource Manual for Secondary Teachers (1982)	2.25
0-8011-0303-7	A Parent's Handbook on California Education (1986)	3.25
0-8011-0671-0	Practical Ideas for Teaching Writing as a Process (1987)	6.00
0-8011-0309-6	Program Guidelines for Hearing Impaired Individuals (1986)	6.00
0-8011-0817-9	Program Guidelines for Language, Speech, and Hearing Specialists Providing Designated Instruction and Services (1989)	6.00
0-8011-0684-2	Program Guidelines for Visually Impaired Individuals (1987)	6.00
0-8011-0815-2	A Question of Thinking: A First Look at Students' Performance on Open-ended Questions in Mathematics (1989)	6.00
0-8011-0311-8	Recommended Readings in Literature, K—8 (1986)	2.25
0-8011-0745-8	Recommended Readings in Literature, K—8, Annotated Edition (1988)	4.50
0-8011-0820-9	Resource Guide: Conferences, Workshops, and Training Opportunities for District and County Business Office Staff, 1989-90 Edition (1989)	4.50
0-8011-0753-9	Respectfully Yours: Magda Gerber's Approach to Professional Infant/Toddler Care (videocassette and guide) (1988)*	65.00
0-8011-0214-6	School Attendance Improvement: A Blueprint for Action (1983)	2.75
0-8011-0189-1	Science Education for the 1980s (1982)	2.50
0-8011-0339-8	Science Framework for California Public Schools (1978)	3.00
0-8011-0354-1	Science Framework Addendum (1984)	3.00
0-8011-0665-6	Science Model Curriculum Guide, K—8 (1987)	3.25
0-8011-0668-0	Science Safety Handbook for California High Schools (1987)	8.75
0-8011-0803-9	Secondary Textbook Review: Biology and Life Science (1989)	10.75
0-8011-0738-5	Secondary Textbook Review: English (1988)	9.25
0-8011-0677-x	Secondary Textbook Review: General Mathematics (1987)	6.50
0-8011-0781-4	Selected Financial and Related Data for California Public Schools (1988)	3.00
0-8011-0752-0	Space to Grow: Creating a Child Care Environment for Infants and Toddlers (videocassette and guide) (1988)*	65.00
0-8011-0265-0	Standards for Scoliosis Screening in California Public Schools (1985)	2.50
0-8011-0486-6	Statement on Preparation in Natural Science Expected of Entering Freshmen (1986)	2.50
0-8011-0318-5	Students' Rights and Responsibilities Handbook (1986)	2.75
0-8011-0234-0	Studies on Immersion Education: A Collection for U.S. Educators (1984)	5.00
0-8011-0682-6	Suicide Prevention Program for California Public Schools (1987)	8.00
0-8011-0778-4	Survey of Academic Skills, Grade 12: Rationale and Content for English—Language Arts (1989)	2.50
0-8011-0785-7	Survey of Academic Skills, Grade 8: Rationale and Content for Mathematics (1989)	2.50
0-8011-0808-x	Survey of Academic Skills, Grade 12: Rationale and Content for Mathematics (1989)	2.50
0-8011-0739-3	Survey of Academic Skills, Grade 8: Rationale and Content for Science (1988)	2.50
0-8011-0827-6	Technical Assistance Manual for the California Model School Accountability Report Card (1989)	3.75
0-8011-0192-1	Trash Monster Environmental Education Kit (for grade six)	23.00
0-8011-0236-7	University and College Opportunities Handbook (1984)	3.25
0-8011-0758-x	Visions for Infant/Toddler Care: Guidelines for Professional Caregivers (1988)	5.50
0-8011-0805-5	Visual and Performing Arts Framework for California Public Schools (1989)	6.00
0-8011-0237-5	Wet 'n' Safe: Water and Boating Safety, Grades 4—6 (1983)	2.50
0-8011-0194-8	Wizard of Waste Environmental Education Kit (for grade three)	20.00
0-8011-0670-2	Work Experience Education Instructional Guide (1987)	12.50
0-8011-0464-5	Work Permit Handbook (1985)	6.00
0-8011-0832-2	Writing Achievement of California Eighth Graders: Year Two (1989)	4.00
0-8011-0686-9	Year-round Education: Year-round Opportunities—A Study of Year-round Education in California (1987)	5.00
0-8011-0270-7	Young and Old Together: A Resource Directory of Intergenerational Resources (1986)	3.00

Orders should be directed to:

California State Department of Education
P.O. Box 271
Sacramento, CA 95802-0271

Please include the International Standard Book Number (ISBN) for each title ordered.

Remittance or purchase order must accompany order. Purchase orders without checks are accepted only from governmental agencies. Sales tax should be added to all orders from California purchasers.

A complete list of publications available from the Department, including apprenticeship instructional materials, may be obtained by writing to the address listed above or by calling (916) 445-1260.

*Videocassette also available in Chinese (Cantonese) and Spanish at the same price.

Order Form

Date _____

Name _____

Address _____

_____
City   State   ZIP code

Title and date of publication	ISBN	Number of copies	Price per copy	Total
Recommended Literature, Grades Nine Through Twelve (1989)	0-8011-0831-4		$4.50	

Make checks payable to:
California State Department of Education

California residents add sales tax $ _____

Total amount $ _____

Mail to:
California State Department of Education
P.O. Box 271
Sacramento, CA 95802-0271

NOTE: Remittance or purchase order must accompany order. Purchase orders without checks are accepted only from governmental agencies.

86-194 (03-0362 and 903-0108) 79687 300 11-89 25M